# Walking in Your Life's Purpose

## The Power of DIP
## Destiny, Identity, and Purpose

BARBARA WENTROBLE

First Printing 2022
ISBN: 9798780257349

Cover Design
David Guillen Velasco

# DEDICATION

My prayer is that the generations to follow me will fulfill their God-given destiny. I also pray that they will leave a legacy for the generations that follow them. God planned for each generation to extend His Kingdom in a greater way than the previous generation was able to do.

With that desire deep in my heart,
I lovingly dedicate this book to:

**My grandchildren:**
Lindsey Wentroble
Annaliese Wentroble
Anna Kooiman
Gabriella Kooiman
Benjamin Kooiman
Kailee Wentroble
Sylvia Wentroble
Ryland Wentroble

**Young generation:**
I also dedicate this book to the young generation arising around the world. May history books record that the world became a better place because you lived!

# CONTENTS

# FOREWORD

I once got lost in the Negev desert in Israel. I was on a quest to find a pillar of salt that is believed to be the remains of Lots' wife. Somewhere in midday, as the sun beat mercilessly, I realized I was running out of water and gas. Even though I had a map, I was lost. Worse yet, I dragged my wife Annabelle with me, and she was seven months pregnant with our first child. We started praying, and after a few more desperate detours into the wasteland, I saw a cloud of dirt off in the distance. I raced our vehicle toward the ground and discovered a jeep. To my immense relief, I found a tour guide. I learned then that a guide is better than a map.

Jesus said, "...it is to your advantage that I go." He knew that the Holy Spirit would come to dwell in believers and guide them into all truth. It is to this end that Jesus sent anointed teachers into the church. They are gifted to train you to hear and follow the guidance of the Spirit. Barbara Wentroble is exceptionally talented in teaching you about Life Purpose.

Can you think of a more critical subject? What makes Barbara exceptional is the fact that she has lived it. In a sense, Barbara is a prophetic guide who has written a map to help you move quickly down a path she spent many years exploring in advance of your arrival. She can show you where the quicksands are and help you avoid dead ends. She will guide you to hidden treasures of wisdom and knowledge in chapters dealing with subjects like

Breaking Generational Curses, Defeating Jezebel and Controlling Spirits, Dreams and Visions that Reveal Your Destiny, Convergence of Your Past and Future to Fulfill Your Destiny, Relationships That Shape Your Destiny, and Spiritual Alignment for Your Life's Assignment. And that's a sample!

Trust me when I say these chapters are gems mined out of a life that has navigated through the territory you are trying to sort out right now. For many of you, Barbara Wentroble is the guide in the Negev that you've been praying for.

**Dr. Lance Wallnau**
**CEO Lance Learning Group**

# INTRODUCTION

Destiny! Identity! Purpose! Someone referred to these words as **DIP**. I like that! I want us to take a DIP into these words that we often hear in today's world. The words destiny, identity and purpose sound wonderful! They seem to motivate us to rise and conquer the world!

At least they seem to do that only for the moment. Within a matter of hours, or even minutes, discouragement, confusion and even helplessness seem to take the place of the excitement from the sound of those powerful words.

"What happened?" you ask yourself. "Maybe this idea of having a destiny in life only applies to *some* people, just not me! After all, I cannot name a single person in my family who did anything significant in life. Likewise, I can't recall anyone in my family who accumulated a sizable amount of wealth, and the ones who had even a small amount of wealth always lost it. Is there a way I can overcome the obstacles in life and move toward a better tomorrow than what I am experiencing today?"

I am so glad you asked! Life is not always easy. It comes with losses, brokenness and wrong mindsets. There are spiritual, physical and emotional battles along life's journey. Dream-destroyers attempt to steal the dreams you have for your life. Negative voices are loud enough to possibly convince you to stop pursuing any measure of success. Life may not be easy, but life *can* be filled with God's purpose! Your life *can* reach the destiny God has planned for you. I wrote this book to encourage you along your life's path. If you are the only person who reaches their destiny after reading this book, I will consider this book a success! My heart is to come alongside you as you move forward. You are on your way to an exciting journey of *Walking in Your Life's Purpose.*

The scriptures taken from The Passion Translation and The Message Bible are not word-for-word translations like traditional Bibles. They are paraphrase versions meant to bring a current day clarity to the scriptures. The publishers who worked on the translations wanted to have a version that communicates to our contemporary society. So, you will see references for those translations (TPT and TMB, respectively) throughout this book, for which you may research those same scriptures in your traditional Bible for comparison.

You are about to discover the reason God put you on Earth. You will realize who you really are, not who your emotions or life have convinced you who you are. After reading this book, you will be certain that you have a purpose in life. You will be empowered to fulfill your destiny and bring glory to the Lord! Generations are waiting for you to become who God made you to be and do what He created you to do. Your time to move forward is now! So, I want to strongly encourage and wholeheartedly say to you, *"Go for it!"*

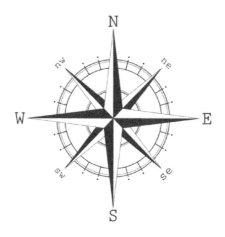

# CHAPTER 1

# From Purpose to Destiny

Recently, I had a discussion with my granddaughter, Kailee. Looking at her, I said, "You work with middle school children at church. What is the main thing these young people want to know?" Kailee quickly responded, "They want to know their purpose in life. They also want to know their identity."

I was amazed at Kailee's keen insight! "That is the same thing 70-year-olds want to know," I replied. I suddenly realized that many people live their entire lives without knowing who they really are. They don't know their purpose in life. These people merely live their lives one day at a time.

Inside these believers is a hunger to understand why they are on the Earth. "Why did God choose to put me on the Earth at this time in history? Why do I need to know my purpose?" You may be asking the same questions.

Knowing your life's purpose breaks you out of the limitations of the past and releases you into the limitless possibilities of your future.

## Limitations that hinder

There are several limitations that hinder a person from walking in their life's purpose. I will only mention a few.

## 1. Victim mindset

A victim mindset is a major hindrance to walking in your purpose. The person believes that they are limited by economics, family background, race, education, or another situation. They can be convinced life favors some people, but others must accept their "lot in life," meaning they must learn to merely *get through life*. How sad!

I love the story of George Washington Carver. He was an agricultural scientist born in the United States in the early 1860s into slavery. As a child, Carver knew very little about his mother or father, as they both died when he was an infant.

However, Carver didn't allow a victim mindset to stop him from pursuing his purpose in life. He could have continued with a mindset of being a slave. He could have seen himself as an orphan. He could have embraced a mindset that he was not qualified to do anything meaningful in life. An old mindset would have stopped Carver in his pursuit of purpose and the fulfillment of his destiny in life.

Carver moved forward to break any old mindset designed to hinder him from walking in his purpose and fulfilling his destiny. After he was freed from slavery, he attended college. He became an inventor of many products and techniques for agriculture. His most famous inventions demonstrated the many uses of peanuts. Whenever I eat peanut butter, I think about George Washington Carver. Aren't you thankful that Carver didn't allow a victim mindset concerning his past to stop him in pursuit of his life's purpose?

## 2. Lack of vision

People who walk in their life's purpose usually must *create* the future they want. They cannot simply accept life as it comes their way. There needs to be a vision for the future. A lack of vision causes the person to merely endure the present. "Where there is no vision, the people are unrestrained" (Proverbs 29:18). Lack of vision causes a person to go backward and never step into the destiny that God has planned for them.

God spoke to Abraham about his destiny. He told Abraham to allow his eyes to see the future God had for him. Abraham needed to see beyond his past and receive a vision of his future.

> The Lord said to Abram, after Lot had separated from him, "Now lift up your eyes and look from the place where you are, northward and southward and eastward and westward; for all the land which you see, I will give it to you and to your descendants forever."
>
> Genesis 13:14-15

Abraham could not possess what he could not see. He needed to look up toward Heaven and allow God to give him fresh vision for his future. Reaching our God-ordained purpose in life is linked with the ability to see God's plan for our future.

Destiny asks the question, "What does the picture of your future look like?" Abraham could have simply looked at his circumstances in life. He could have looked at his earthly family background. Generations before him lived in a pagan land, and none of his relatives were godly people. Why would God use someone with his background to do anything significant in life? You may be asking the same question about your life. Your family background may have hindered you from having a fresh vision for your future. Why would God use you to do anything significant on Earth?

Embracing your purpose involves the ability to see, through God's eyes, the future He has for you, your family, your ministry, or your business. Everyone has a purpose, but not everyone walks in it. Once your eyes are open to the ultimate plan for your life, you begin to experience transformation in your thoughts, emotions, energy level, and your actions.

## 3. Fear

Another hindrance to walking in your life's purpose is fear. I love the acronym for FEAR: False Evidence Appearing Real. The primary stronghold in my childhood and early adult life was fear. I was afraid of everything! I feared speaking to people. I feared I would fail in every venture I undertook. I feared lack of finances. You name it, and I probably had that fear!

The Lord was gracious to me and helped me break out of those lifelong fears. With the help of the Lord, I learned to run into those fears and not run away from them. I had to willingly choose to do what I didn't want to do. When I didn't want to speak to people, I had to choose to lean on the Lord and speak anyway. When I began a new business venture or any other pursuit, I had to take a risk and do it anyway, despite being afraid. When I feared financial failure, I learned that giving finances was a weapon to break me out of lack and into financial blessings. I learned to get into the presence of the Lord. I would hear Him speak to my innermost being, and His voice would break the power of negative voices, fears, insecurities, and anything designed to stop me from advancing into my life's purpose.

At that time, I was not aware that all of this was connected to my purpose and to my destiny. However, I learned, as many of you may have, "our pain becomes our platform!" My purpose in these situations was to give me experience and preparation to fulfill my destiny. How little, during those times, did I understand my destiny. I did not know that God was preparing me to speak internationally, to step out in business and ministry ventures, and to equip other people for freedom from poverty and lack. Writing books and ministering to an international audience was beyond my comprehension. I had to look to the Lord, receive His vision for my future, and run into every fear that raised its ugly head!

The Passion Bible encourages us as we break out of the old cycle of hindrances designed to keep us from our destiny.

> You did not receive the "spirit of religious duty," leading you back into the fear *of never being good enough*. But you have received the "Spirit of full acceptance," enfolding you into the family of God. And you will never feel orphaned, for as he rises up within us, our spirits join him in saying the words of tender affection, "Beloved Father!" For the Holy Spirit makes God's fatherhood real to us as he whispers into our innermost being, "You are God's beloved child!"
>
> Romans 8:15-17 TPT

**Discovering my purpose**

Reflecting over my life, I see how the Lord guided my life and circumstances toward my ultimate purpose. I grew up in a family as the eldest of six children. Throughout my young life, I helped my mother care for my sisters and brothers. It seemed that I was always in charge and assigning them the chores that needed to be done.

Then, during my years as a student nurse, I helped mentor other nursing students in chemistry and various subjects. I did not want them to fail. I volunteered and stayed awake many nights to be sure that they succeeded. Ministry has always involved encouraging and coaching others to rise to their destiny. That is simply a normal part of my life.

Over the years, the pieces of my life's puzzle began to come together. When I knew I was called into ministry, I finally understood my life purpose from God! I often describe my purpose as: *Empowering others to fulfill their dreams and help them create wealth to fulfill their life's purpose.* Once I discovered my life's purpose, I found myself energized for whatever came my way. I also understood that the fulfillment of my purpose was a *process*, which would ultimately lead me to my destiny.

**Passion defines purpose.**
Discovering my purpose ignited my life in a new way. I understood why I was passionate about empowering others for their life's purpose. My passion defined my purpose! If you are not passionate about something, it is probably not your purpose. Passion will also cause you to desire significance by creating a legacy for future generations. Your purpose is not merely about yourself. Your purpose always involves others.

God is the God of generations. In the Bible, He refers to Himself as the God of Abraham, Isaac, and Jacob. These men represented three generations. Therefore, God is the God who created a legacy by causing His blessings to flow through the generations. His desire is for us to be like Him and see that our purpose is generational!

**A life of significance**
Purpose will cause you to tolerate the present but live in the future. You will spend your life working for something greater than your own life. You will be passionate to live a life of significance. However, a life of significance is not usually a life of ease. It often involves overcoming pain and adversity. Life today is, unfortunately, filled with economic and social upheavals, sickness, and broken relationships, many of which you must face-off and overcome, keeping your focus on the future to obtain a life of significance.

God has a people who refuse to stop despite the adversities of life. They are part of a small group of people who march to the sound of a different drummer! They realize that difficulty is the womb of creativity. They can take the lemons in life and use them to create lemonade. It is time for you to set up your own lemonade stand! Use every sour circumstance in your life and allow the Lord to create something sweet out of it. Your pain will become your platform.

Your platform is your ability to influence the lives of others. Receive the empowerment to live each day filled with God's divine purpose for your life. You are not where you will be in the future, as your past should not limit your future. Failures, disappointments, wrong decisions, and many other negative issues may be part of your past. Yet, with the help of the Lord, those situations cannot keep you from achieving the best God has for your future. He has planned a great future for you. Refuse to just allow life to happen. Refuse any victim mindset that wants to keep you in an old place. Keep moving forward and see the Lord bring you into your divine purpose. You were created for this time! Be empowered for your God-given purpose!

> Thus says the Lord, "Restrain your voice from weeping, And your eyes from tears; For your work shall be rewarded," declares the Lord, "And they shall return from the land of the enemy. And there is hope for your future," declares the Lord.
>
> Jeremiah 31:16-17

# DISCUSSION QUESTIONS

1. How has a victim mindset limited you in life?
2. Describe a fear that you had to overcome.
3. What is the vision that you have for your future?

4. Describe the passion in your heart.
5. How are you pursuing your passion?

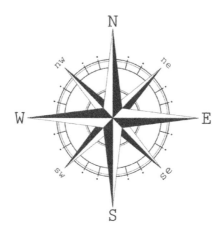

# CHAPTER 2

# Receiving My True Identity

Preschool and kindergarten children get excited when they learn to write their names. John. Ben. Sue. Linda. These young people want everyone to know they can write their names. They get excited when they can recognize the spelling of their names! Later, they want to know more about themselves than only name recognition. They begin to have questions about their identity.

Who am I? Why am I on Earth? People of all ages frequently ask these questions. Much discussion is taking place today over identity. People want to know their true identity. For example, some people "sense" they are one gender identity today and another gender identity the next day. A term is used for the confusion in gender identity.

> **Gender dysphoria (GD)** is the distress a person experiences due to a mismatch between their gender identity—their personal sense of their own gender—and their sex assigned at birth. The diagnostic label **gender identity disorder (GID)** was used until 2013 with the release of the diagnostic manual DSM-5. The condition was renamed to remove the stigma associated with the term *disorder*.[1]

The Bible reveals God's plan for mankind's gender. When God created mankind, there was no fluidity of gender. God saw His creation of male and female and declared that it was very good. (See Genesis 1:31.) He had the best plan for mankind. "God created man in His own image, in the image of God He created him; male and female He created them" (Genesis 1:27).

People everywhere are longing to know their true identity. The Bible tells us Earth is also desiring the same thing! Creation longs for God's people to know their identity and to walk in it.

> For the anxious longing of the creation waits eagerly for the revealing of the sons of God.
> Romans 8:19 TPT

The entire universe is standing on tiptoe, yearning to see the unveiling of God's glorious sons and daughters!

---

[1] https://en.Wikipedia.org/wiki/Gender_dysphoria, 2022, online.

## God's dream

Before time began, God dreamed of having a big family of Sons and Daughters. He was not satisfied with having a small family. He did not want only a few people who looked to Him as Father. He is a big God. He likes big!

I came from a big family. As I mentioned previously, there were six siblings along with my two parents. We lived in a house with three bedrooms. The four sisters shared one bedroom. We had to learn to get along, since we lived in such tight surroundings! Today, we are older and live in different cities and different parts of the United States. We still love each other and prioritize times when we can get together. Big families can be a blessing.

God's dream of a big family started before you were born. In fact, God's dream began before anything was created. Before the stars were created, before the sun and moon were created, before He created Earth and time began, you were in the mind, thoughts, and intents of God. He dreamed of a big family. He wanted Sons and Daughters who would look like Him and act like Him. You were in His heart before you were in the hearts of your parents.

## Meeting in Heaven

God had a meeting in Heaven to plan for your life before He created His family. Many couples today plan for their families. Some want a few children. Others want a larger family. These couples often plan for the number of children they want. Sometimes, a child is born who was not planned. However, God plans for all children. You are not an accident. You are not a mistake. The circumstances for your birth may not have been convenient, yet God planned for each child who comes to Earth.

God's plan for your life happened in that meeting in Heaven before time began. I sometimes describe the meeting like a Board Meeting. In the room in Heaven, I visualize a long conference table. Around the table is God the Father, God the Son, and God the Holy Spirit.

The special agenda for the meeting was to discuss your life. Details of your life were planned by the Godhead at that time. Words were spoken about you: words about your identity, words concerning your life's purpose, words about your destiny, your gender, your skin color, and all the intricate parts of your life. All were spoken!

During this meeting, a Book was written to document your life. All the words spoken concerning your purpose and your destiny were written in that book. The Old Testament calls the book the Volume of the Book. The New Testament names it the Book of Life. Your name was written in the book. In the United States, government agencies record a person's birth. Before civil governments documented your birth, Heaven recorded your name in the Book of Life. This Book of Life, with your name in it, was written before time began!

In the fullness of God's appointed time, He formed you in your mother's womb. He fashioned you and made you into the child He wanted you to be.

> For You formed my inward parts; You wove me in my mother's womb. I will give thanks to You, for I am fearfully and wonderfully made; Wonderful are Your works, And my soul knows it very well. My frame was not hidden from You, When I was made in secret, And skillfully wrought in the depths of the earth; Your eyes have seen my unformed substance; And in Your book were all written The days that were ordained for me, When as yet there was not one of them.
>
> Psalm 139:13-16, NASB 1995

The Book of Life recorded your identity and the destiny for your life. God planned the moment He wanted you to enter Earth as His Son or Daughter. He knew that He needed you on Earth at this time.

**We have forgotten the meeting.**
Although God had a powerful meeting in Heaven, you and I have a problem. The problem is we have forgotten the meeting. We forgot the words spoken over us. We forgot the identity and the purpose for our lives. We forgot the words recorded in the Book of Life.

I heard a statement years ago. I don't remember who spoke the words, but I do remember the statement. "If you don't know where you came from, you don't know what you are about." How true!

We must remember where we came from. We came from the heart of God. He is our true Father. He longed to have us as His child and part of His family. We must know what we are about. We are on Earth to fulfill the purpose of God.

**Old identity**
An old identity can hinder a person from fulfilling their destiny. The old identity may not be a person's true identity, as the old identity can be formed through many different influences.

Voices from influential people impact a person in a strong way. Those influential people may be a person's parents, peers, teachers, or other people the person considers significant. Sometimes a parent can tell the child, "You are bad!" The child grows up thinking they are a bad person. The parent may not have separated the child from the deed. If the child did something wrong, the *action* may have been wrong, but the child is still good. Often, these parents were treated the same way when they were growing up. They may still be carrying the pain of their own childhood and not realize what they are doing to the child's developing identity and perspective of themselves.

A teacher can tell the person they are stupid or a failure. Teachers have a great impact on a child. The child may then grow up thinking they are not bright enough to learn. They consider themselves as "stupid."

You may be remembering a significant person who spoke negative words over your life. Forgive the person for the pain that went into you when you heard those words. Turn them over to the Lord. Ask Him to heal those people from the pain that is causing them to hurt others.

## Occupation

Another influence that affects a person's identity is their occupation. Sometimes when a person is asked who they are, they reply with their role at work. "I am a doctor." "I am an engineer." "I am a teacher."

The person believes their occupation defines who they are. That is one reason many people are depressed or confused when the job ends through an unexpected firing or retirement. Their identity was in the occupation. When the occupation is gone, they don't know who they are.

## Circumstances

One more influence that affects a person's identity can be circumstances. A person growing up in poverty can see their identity as "poor." The person can't see the potential in themselves to break out of lack. They feel their life is doomed to never having enough. They hoard clothes and food for a "rainy day."

Often people who have experienced any kind of abuse identify themselves as a victim. Whatever happens in life is a result of them being a victim. The sad part is often the person goes from one abusive situation to another. They seem drawn to abusive people. God has a way for these people to be free and come into their true identity!

## True identity

Your true identity breaks you out of the limitations of the past and releases you into the limitless, glorious possibilities of your future. The time for you to step out of an old identity and step into your true identity is now. We are in a NOW season!

**You are beginning to remember.** Understanding that you are, at your core, essentially a spirit, and realizing that helps in knowing your identity. "He who is joined to the Lord is one spirit with Him" (1 Corinthians 6:17 NKJV). "That which is born of the flesh is flesh, and that which is born of the Spirit is spirit" (John 3:6). Remembering your identity and who you really are sometimes happens during a dream, or you may suddenly have a vision. You may even remember a prophetic word. These dreams, visions, and prophetic words often speak of your true identity. If we are not careful, we will either ignore or push down those occurrences. Our mind can tell us we could never be that way. We can never do what we saw ourselves doing in those spiritual encounters. However, a person must be willing to listen to those dreams, visions, and prophetic words, since they are reminding us about the Meeting in Heaven. They are causing us to remember words spoken over us before time began and helping us understand our true identity as a "chosen one."

You were chosen by God before you ever entered this world. He chose you before you ever did one deed. He did not choose you because of some great action you performed. He chose you because of His great love.

> Even as [in His love] He chose us [actually picked us out for Himself as His own] in Christ before the foundation of the world, that we should be holy (consecrated and set apart for Him) and blameless in His sight, even above reproach, before Him in love.
>
> Ephesians 1:4 AMPCE

> Long before he laid down earth's foundations, he had us in mind, had settled on us as the focus of his love, to be made whole and holy by his love.
>
> Ephesians 1:4 MSG

God's love is breaking His offspring into freedom from every hindering situation. No longer are God's Sons and Daughters slaves to sin and flesh! No longer are they clothed with guilt and condemnation! Their conscience has been cleansed by the Blood of the Lamb. Past sins are forgiven and placed in the Sea of Forgetfulness. (See Micah 7:19.) They are now conscious of the presence of the Lord and His Kingdom purposes.

Embrace your true identity as a "chosen one" by the Lord. You were created to fulfill God's Kingdom purpose on Earth. His love for you is more powerful than the circumstances of your earthly past. Enjoy being who you were created to be before time began!

# DISCUSSION QUESTIONS

1. Describe the meeting in Heaven when God planned for your life.
2. What are some old identities that are currently defining who you are?
3. Where did those identities come from?
4. What are some dreams, visions, or prophetic words you have received about your life?
5. How can you begin to walk in your new identity?

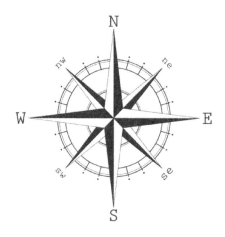

# CHAPTER 3

# The Battle to Become
# Who I Really Am

I seldom watch movies. Instead, I would rather read a book. However, there are a few movies I have watched that made an impact on my life. *Seabiscuit* is one of them. The movie is based on a true story.

In the movie, Seabiscuit is a horse that had many obstacles to overcome before he received his true identity as a champion thoroughbred racehorse. His natural physique would normally disqualify him immediately for anything significant in the horseracing industry.

Seabiscuit was described as lazy and small in stature, as well as having wobbly knees. Early in his racing years, he lost many of the competitions. He probably didn't sense the potential on the inside of himself. Seabiscuit may have developed the mindset of a mediocre horse that could only watch others achieve greatness in life.

Positive and encouraging words from trainers and owners were interjected into Seabiscuit all along his journey as he developed into his true identity. Eventually, a special trainer, who was known for his unusual training methods, was given the task of working with Seabiscuit. Instinctively, he somehow knew a hidden potential was inside this horse.

With the help of a good rider and a great trainer, Seabiscuit was on a path to his true identity! He could no longer excuse his physical build or his tendency to lay around and waste time. He could no longer listen to past negative voices that told him he was a failure. As with all of us throughout our lives, obstacles must be overcome. Personality defects must change. Seabiscuit, too, had to listen to the positive voices and overcome the challenges he faced. He was destined to be a winner and not a failure!

What a winner he was! He earned the title of "Horse of the Year" in 1938. His successes brought in enormous wealth.[1] Seabiscuit first needed to realize and embrace his true identity in order to fulfill his destiny. Battles, such as his physique, his wobbly knees, his perception of himself, and his lack of determination, had to be fought and won before he could leave such an unforgettable legacy for future generations.

---

[1] https://thecinemaholic.com/the-inspiring-story-behind-seabiscuit-explained

**Battles to be fought**

God's people must also fight and win battles in their pursuit of true identity. God's will for our lives is not automatic. Obstacles along life's path seek to deter you from your identity and destiny. These obstacles can hinder you in becoming who you are meant to be, or they can be a steppingstone to your future.

I read the story about someone named Dolly Conner. She was born with small optic nerves. Her eyesight was limited in both eyes. The story records Dolly's inability to drive a car, read a magazine, or the ability to read from a chalkboard.

Dolly was willing to fight the battle of limited physical vision. Still, she played backup center for the Monmouth College basketball team. Even though she had very limited vision, she acquired the ability to shoot a basketball through the hoop! Her scores were amazing![2] Dolly fought the battle of overcoming limited vision and won the victory! She secured a true identity in becoming a successful basketball player!

**Battleground of the mind**

The greatest battle people fight is the battle in their minds. The enemy has blinded the minds of many people from the truth of who God made them to be. He tries to convince God's people they are someone or something less than God's glorious creation. These minds fail to remember the covenant God has promised for them.

When a person receives Jesus as their Savior, they step into covenant with God who never forgets and never breaks covenant. Covenant is the agreement between two parties. The two parties are committed to their relationship. Today, some people use the word covenant to describe a relationship. Yet, many times the use of that word becomes frivolous. When hard times come, the person walks away from the relationship.

---

[2] Glenn Van Ekeren, *Speaker's Sourcebook II, Quotes, Stories, and Anecdotes for Every Occasion* (New York, NY: Penguin Putnam, Inc., 1994), p. 270.

God is not that way! When you are in covenant with the Lord, He keeps covenant with you! As believers, we are in relationship with God. Therefore, we are in covenant with Him. His promise of covenant is a reminder to our minds of His faithfulness to us. "Remember His covenant forever, the word which He commanded to a thousand generations" (1 Chronicles 16:15).

Our minds often try to convince us that God does not love us. They attempt to convince us that we are not worthy of His forgiveness. Our minds can even persuade us we don't deserve a relationship with the Lord. How sad! Our minds have either forgotten, or they doubt, the faithfulness of God's covenant. Our minds are battlefields and can keep us from our true identity as a loved child of God.

> In reference to your former manner of life, you
> lay aside the old self, which is being corrupted in
> accordance with the lusts of deceit, and that you
> be renewed in the spirit of your mind.
> Ephesians 4:22-23, NASB 1995

How wonderful to know our minds can be renewed to the faithfulness of a covenant-keeping God!

## Doubt

Another battle that keeps a person from his or her true identity is the battle against doubt. Doubt attempts to keep a person in an old place. The person believes the way they are today is the way they will always be. Scriptures and prophetic words may be accurate for some people. Just not me!

I remember the first prophetic word I received. I was new in the spirit-filled walk with the Lord. I was so excited with the reality of God who loves me and talks with me. Every day was filled with the joy of experiencing His presence. My husband and I went to every believer's meeting we heard about!

In one of those meetings, the speaker asked me to come forward. I still have the memory of the sanctuary in that church. The memory has never faded. The speaker spoke prophetic words over me. I was not familiar with prophecy, but somehow, I knew those were words from the Lord.

"You will stand before kings and rulers in nations. You will deliver words from the Lord to those leaders." What powerful words! The words sounded wonderful. Then, doubt entered my mind. How could I ever do that? At that time in my life, I was helpless to speak to even a few people. How could I ever speak to such high-level leaders in nations? Not only that, how would I even get to other nations? People didn't frequently fly around the world the way we do today. Doubt of my identity as an international speaker flooded my mind and emotions.

For many years, I pondered that prophetic word. I knew it was God's word. Yet, I doubted the word could ever manifest in my life. Who was I? I saw my identity as a young mother of three children. I did not speak in public. I had not attended Bible School. I was unqualified to possess the identity spoken over me.

Today, however, I am doing the very thing that was prophesied over me so long ago. But first, I had to battle the enemy's seed of doubt concerning God's prophetic word over my life in order to possess my true identity. I remember the years spent resisting doubt. I devoured every verse in my Bible. I put my name in scriptures to help me embrace my true identity. I submitted my life to the Lord on a daily basis. Little by little, I won the battle against doubt of my true identity.

Many Bible characters fought the same battle of doubt I fought. Gideon was one of them. He was hiding in a winepress, beating out wheat. The Angel of the Lord visited this fearful man. He lived in fear due to the defeated battles in the past with the Midianites. The Angel spoke to Gideon's potential and not to his present condition of fear.

"The Lord is with you, valiant warrior" (Judges 6:12). This prophetic word spoke to Gideon's true identity, not to who he thought he was. Although the Angel of the Lord, the

Preincarnate Jesus, spoke truth, doubt entered Gideon's mind. He began questioning his new identity. Gideon reminded the Angel of the attacks his nation had experienced. He questioned the lack of supernatural miracles among his people. He reminded the Angel of the Lord about his family being the least in the nation. He was the youngest and the least qualified. Yet, the Angel assured him that he was the deliverer God had chosen. Gideon had to overcome the battle of doubt and believe God's word for his true identity. Once he overcame his doubt, he was able to wear his true identity as a victorious warrior.

Facing the battle of doubt is necessary in receiving a true identity. Have you received a prophetic word and yet doubted the reality of that word? Is doubt hindering you from walking in your true identity? Demand now that doubt leaves your mind! Ask the Lord to free you from all doubt and unbelief. Ask Him to fill you with faith to possess who He made you to be!

## Uncertain future

Another battle that many people fight is the battle to overcome an uncertain future. The initial desire to embrace a true identity can be exciting. A person may have listened to a speaker, read a book, and written the steps needed to move forward. The plan is in place. Then, life happens! A relationship is broken. Sickness comes. Finances are lost. Hope for the future turns into despair.

Facing an uncertain future can leave a person feeling unstable and insecure. The internal battle rages as thoughts, emotions, and visions of the future bombard a person's mind. *How is it possible now to step forward in my true identity and fulfill God's destiny for my life? Maybe some other time? Maybe never. It is too late for me. I am too old to start over.*

These questions and comments are all too familiar to many people. An uncertain future stops many believers in their pursuit of God's purpose and destiny for their lives. When a spouse or loved one dies, the future looks uncertain. Often, the person who dies was part of the plan for the future.

I remember a friend who lost a husband. They were both pastors of a local church. The wife was a powerful minister alongside her husband. When the husband died suddenly, not only did the wife experience pain, but the entire congregation was hurting. The wife told me how she would cry all week long over the loss. On Sunday, she had to ignore her own grief, step into her identity as a pastor, and release healing to the congregation. The uncertain future loomed in front of her for an entire year. Yet, she kept pressing into her true identity, as a Daughter of the Lord. She realized that He had given her the courage and strength to fulfill her assignment on Earth. Today, the congregation is whole and growing in their walk with the Lord. The minister disciples the congregation, while discipling those in other nations, too. She did not allow an uncertain future to steal the plan of God for her life.

The loss of a job or loss of income can paint the picture of an uncertain future. Economic loss can create a fierce battle for most people. The future usually looks uncertain and can look hopeless. A person wonders how they can step into their future when the future looks so bleak. Sleepless nights are spent trying to develop a mental strategy to keep from losing all the person has worked for. No time *now* for pursuing identity! The pursuit of paying the mortgage, buying food, and keeping the family together overtakes any thoughts of a bright future.

I remember a friend who was working to build a financial base for his life. He had a passion for ministering to others. Yet, he needed finances for him and his wife to provide the necessities of life. The friend decided he would pursue getting professional credibility to start a counseling business.

After taking a course in counseling, he was required to pass a test. Passing the test would give him the credentials needed for his business. One afternoon, I received a phone call from him with an update on his progress. My friend told me that, sadly, he failed the test. Then, he began to question everything! *What should I do? Maybe the counseling business was really not for me.*

*Maybe the identity of a counselor must not be part of my destiny. After all, I failed the test!*

As we continued to dialogue over the phone, I remember asking my friend how many times he could take the test. As he paused, it was like, "Whoa! Wait a minute! Yes!" He could take the test again, and again, and again if needed! He then realized one failed test would not stop his pursuit of destiny. As we ended the call, he agreed to restudy and retake the test.

The battle was on! My friend knew he was fighting a battle for his true identity. God did not create him for failure! He was created as a Son of God with a destiny to fulfill.

Today, my friend has multiple certificates for various aspects of counseling. Government offices send clients to him. Various agencies send clients to him. Why do they do this? They do it because he is the best counselor and gets the most results of anyone in his territory.

The uncertain future tried to stop my friend from becoming the successful person God made him to be. The failed test was a battle weapon used to convince my friend that he could never fulfill his assignment from the Lord. But God!

Look your uncertain future in the face! Decree who you really are, not what life's happening tries to tell you who you are. You are the Son or Daughter of the Most High God. His plans and purposes can be fulfilled in your life. I love what Ted Levitt says: "The future belongs to people who see possibilities before they become obvious."[3] In the midst of your uncertain future, look at the possibilities at the end of your battle!

**Battles are real.**
The battles to secure your true identity are real! I have only mentioned a few. Whenever these painful and fearful battles come, realize the source of the battle. Understand that each

---

[3] Glenn Van Ekeren, *Speaker's Source Book II, Quotes, Stories, and Anecdotes for Every Occasion* (New York, NY: Penguin Putnam, Inc., 1994), p. 167.

battle is designed to steal your true identity and hinder you from fulfilling God's purpose and destiny for your life.

You were born to be a winner. You were born to bear the image of the Father on Earth. The last chapter of your life has not been written. Keep moving forward into your future. You were born for this time in history!

## DISCUSSION QUESTIONS

1. Describe a battle in your mind that you had to overcome.
2. What is a covenant relationship?
3. Discuss a prophetic word that was spoken over your life.
4. What are you doing with that prophetic word from the Lord?
5. How do you deal with doubt concerning God's plan for your life?

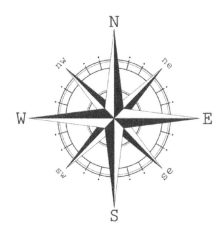

# CHAPTER 4

# Breaking Generational Curses

The missionary speaking at our church delivered a great message. I was captivated by the stories he told. He spoke about some of the evil forces he encountered in the nation where he was serving. I was new in my walk with the Holy Spirit, and I had never heard anyone in my church talk about demonic powers. I certainly never heard anything about them causing problems for people today.

I remember being told if a person was not "born again," they would spend eternity in a fiery hell and be tormented by the devil and his demons. But in this life, they were exempt from the powers of darkness.

The missionary began to paint a powerful picture about the reality of demonic power in today's world. Then he said something that shocked me! "These demonic powers operate in other nations. In America, we do not have to deal with this. We are too 'civilized' for demons to bother us."

Somehow, my mind and spirit did not believe this. If the devil and demons were not active in my nation, why was there so much evil operating? Where did murder and crime come from? What is the source of spouse and childhood abuse? Why are many families experiencing divorce? The list of evils went on and on in my mind.

Could the statement about civilized people be true? My mind questioned what I had just heard. If the enemy was not bothering civilized people, then where were all the horrible events in our nation coming from? That day began my journey in seeking truth concerning evil powers.

**Destiny involves warfare**.
Evil powers are an enemy to a person's identity and destiny. The enemy really doesn't care if you read your Bible and pray eight hours each day. He doesn't care if you attend church meetings three times each week. He doesn't care if you have prophetic dreams and visions. What he really wants is for you to miss your destiny!

Why does the devil want you to miss your destiny? Because your destiny is not only about you. It involves the liberation of other people and territories. Some of those people include your family. They may be captive to curses that have been passed down for generations. Your region may not be experiencing the blessings of God. Much of the painful and horrible events people experience are the result of spiritual warfare operating out of curses.

The Apostle Paul was familiar with spiritual warfare. He warned the people in Ephesus about the necessity of being strong in their battles with the enemy.

> And that about wraps it up. God is strong, and he wants you strong. So take everything the Master has set out for you, well-made weapons of the best materials. And put them to use so you will be able to stand up to everything the Devil throws your way. This is no afternoon athletic contest that we'll walk away from and forget about in a couple of hours. This is for keeps, a life-or-death fight to the finish line against the Devil and all his angels.
>
> Be prepared. You're up against far more than you can handle on your own. Take all the help you can get, every weapon God has issued, so that when it's all over but the shouting you'll still be on your feet.
>
> Ephesians 6:10-13 MSG

God in you is strong. He can release supernatural power and authority to help you win the spiritual battles you encounter.

**Spiritual warfare**
We often refer to the battles we face as "spiritual warfare." The word *warfare* comes from a Greek word that means *strategy*. Strategy is needed to defeat the evil powers hindering our destiny and the destiny of our loved ones.

The Apostle Paul reminded the Corinthians about the nature of the battles they faced. Their battle was not with people. The battle was spiritual. Spiritual weapons were necessary in the battle. These spiritual weapons were powerful enough to defeat the enemy.

> For the weapons of our warfare are not of the flesh, but divinely powerful for the destruction of fortresses.
>
> 2 Corinthians 10:4

> For although we live in the natural realm, we don't wage a military campaign employing human weapons, *using manipulation to achieve our aims.* Instead, our *spiritual* weapons are energized with divine power to effectively dismantle the defenses *behind which people hide.*
>
> 2 Corinthians 10:3-4 TPT

The same spiritual weapons Apostle Paul spoke about are needed in the battles believers face today. Individuals, families, and people in territories battle evil, demonic forces. These demonic forces attempt to keep people from fulfilling God's will on Earth. The Bible exhorts believers to resist these enemy powers. "Stand up to the devil and resist him and he will flee in agony" (James 4:7 TPT).

The traditional church I grew up in taught me the devil was defeated. The teaching told me, because I am a Christian, the enemy is defeated and cannot interfere in my life. Later, after reading the Bible and studying the scriptures, I discovered I only knew half of the truth. Yes, the enemy was legally defeated by Jesus. His death, burial, and resurrection defeated the authority of the devil. He still has power, but he does not have authority. However, the enemy is a rebellious law breaker. He is lawless!

God's people on Earth are empowered to reinforce the victory that Jesus won. They are assigned to manage Earth as God's ambassadors. Spiritual weapons are available to us so we can be successful in reaching our God-given destiny. Spiritual weapons have the authority and power to give victory in spiritual battles!

## Causes of spiritual battles

What are some of the causes of these spiritual battles? Too often in today's world, evil powers are accepted as normal. Children's games often involve occultic activity. Television shows portray involvement in psychic activities as a current way of life. Breakdowns in family relationships, emotional instabilities, addictions, and many other painful events plague families and cities. Is there a root cause that has opened the door to these problems?

Very often, the root of many of these problems can be traced to personal or generational curses. Someone disobeyed God and permitted the enemy to plunder the inheritance God had for a family or a territory. Curses may result from personal disobedience to God or passed down from former generations. Unforgiveness, antisemitism, oaths taken in secret societies such as Freemasonry, Eastern Star, and similar groups opens the door to demonic activity. As a result, the family or territory has not been able to fulfill the destiny that God planned for them.

Deuteronomy 28 lists the curses and blessings that can overtake people. Blessings are the result of obedience to the Lord. Curses are the result of disobedience to God.

> Now it shall be, if you will diligently obey the Lord your God, being careful to do all His commandments which I command you today, that the Lord your God will set you high above all the nations of the earth. All these blessings will come upon you and overtake you if you obey the Lord your God.
>
> Deuteronomy 28:1-2

Blessings include our children, prosperity, the work of your hands, favor, and victory over enemies that rise up against us. The Bible also warns about the curses that result from disobedience to God.

> It shall come about, if you will not obey the Lord
> your God, to observe to do all His
> commandments and His statutes with which I
> charge you today, that all these curses shall come
> upon you and overtake you.
>
> Deuteronomy 28:15

Curses can include barrenness, addiction, premature death, poverty, infirmities, broken relationships, and defeat by your enemies. Families and territories often experience the result of curses without knowing why they are experiencing many of these evils. Maybe they are like me when I thought the enemy could not touch me since I was a Christian.

### Keys to break curses

The good news for believers is you can be free from any curse that attempts to steal your destiny and God's purpose for your life! The spiritual weapons available to believers are more powerful than anything the enemy can send your way! I only mention a few of these weapons that are available.

### 1. Blood of Jesus

One of the most powerful weapons used to break curses is the Blood of Jesus. Whenever we take communion, also known as the Lord's Supper, we are repeating our covenant pledge to the Lord. We are enforcing our commitment to the power of Jesus' blood that bought our freedom.

An intellectual understanding of the power of the Blood is not always sufficient to break a curse. Usually, a person needs to appropriate the Blood to their life through prayer and faith. I often pray this way:

> *Lord, I thank You for your Blood that was spilled out at Calvary. I repent for my sins and the sins of former generations in my family. Forgive me and anyone in my bloodline that walked in disobedience to you. You died and rose again so that I could have life everlasting.*

*I decree Your blood has never lost its power. By faith, I apply the Blood to my life. I put the Blood of Jesus between me and all former generations. I break every curse assigned to my family. I receive the cleansing in my life and in my family from all curses.*

## 2. Forgiveness

Forgiveness is another powerful spiritual weapon. It is important to forgive people who have hurt you or done wrong things against you. You are not saying that what they did was right. You are merely turning them over to the Lord.

It is also important to forgive others who left you vulnerable to a curse. People in your bloodline who invited a curse against you need to be forgiven. Unforgiveness opens the door to tormenting spirits, insanity, and many other emotional and mental problems. Unforgiveness is a mean spirit that can affect a person's mind!

Not all mental illness is a demon. Sometimes a person has chemical or other issues that affect them. Abuse, trauma, and many life situations can result in emotional or mental problems. Many people only need healing from their deep wounds. Forgiveness is a medicine that can heal many of these wounds. The cost of unforgiveness is too high not to forgive!

## 3. Name of Jesus

The Name of Jesus is another powerful weapon to break curses. Jesus defeated the powers of darkness through His death, burial, and resurrection. His Name is the name above all other names—including the names of curses. Demons fear His Name!

Unbelievers may try to use the Name of Jesus but do not have the power or authority to invoke His Name. The story in the Bible about the sons of Sceva records the impotence of men who saw the power of the Lord but could not use that power.

Some of the Jewish exorcists, who went from place to place, attempted to name over those who had the evil spirits the name of the Lord

Jesus, saying, "I adjure you by Jesus whom Paul preaches." Seven sons of one Sceva, a Jewish chief priest, were doing this. And the evil spirit answered and said to them, "I recognize Jesus, and I know about Paul, but who are you?" And the man, in whom was the evil spirit, leaped on them and subdued all of them and overpowered them, so that they fled out of that house naked and wounded.

Acts 19:13-16, NASB 1995

It is good to know that unbelievers can see and acknowledge the manifestation of the power of the Name of Jesus. Yet only God's covenant believers can use that weapon to set people free and also to secure their destiny!

## 4. Decrees

Another weapon to break curses is by releasing a decree. A decree is a law or judgment put in place by a ruler. It is an official order, edict, or decision.[1] A person releasing a decree to break curses is a believer representing the Lord on Earth. You carry the identity of God. You have been given the power of the Holy Spirit. Your voice to decree becomes like the voice of the Lord. "You will also decree a thing, and it will be established for you; And light will shine on your ways" (Job 22:28).

Decrees alter the spirit realm so the purposes of God in your life or territory are established on Earth! The ruler, Jesus, has given you as His ambassador, an official order to decree on Earth what He is decreeing in Heaven. You are decreeing God's will for you, your family, or your territory. Keep decreeing the will of God until you see the full manifestation of God's destiny for your life!

---

[1] Michael Agnes, Editor in Chief, *Webster's New World Dictionary, Fourth Edition, Defining the English Language for the 21ˢᵗ Century* (New York, NY: Macmillan USA, 1999), p. 376.

## Authority over curses

Your voice, released in authority, unlocks the power needed for the effective use of spiritual weapons. I wrote about the power of authority in my book, *Praying with Authority*.

> As believers, once we have come under God's authority, we are able to pray with His authority. God speaks to people who are in relationship with Him. He gives them revelation of His will. The revelation of His will releases in believers the authority to speak forth His will in a situation. Therefore, revelation releases authority.[2]

Sometimes I pray and ask the Lord to help me receive the revelation and authority that I need to break curses in my life or in my territory:

> *Lord, I thank you for the privilege of being your ambassador on Earth. My desire is to represent you and your power against all evil curses that affect my destiny. I choose to be your voice and speak as your representative on the Earth. Grant me the courage and authority to speak as You would speak. Grant me the revelation I need to speak as Your representative. I receive Your authority to break curses and release blessings. May You be glorified as I walk in Your divine destiny for my life.*

## Undeserved curse

No one is perfect. At times we do not obey the Lord in every way. That does not always open our lives to a curse. We can repent when we realize we have disobeyed the Lord. Confession and repentance cleanse our hearts and lives. Any undeserved curse sent against you can be broken. Use the same weapons mentioned above to break any undeserved curse.

---

[2] Barbara Wentroble, *Praying with Authority* (Ventura, CA: Regal Books, 2003), p. 25.

Undeserved curses can come from witches, occult persons, unbelievers, or anyone who opposes you and your walk with the Lord. The power and authority given to you by the Lord is stronger than anything the enemy uses against you. It is also stronger than the fear that attempts to stop you from breaking curses. The Bible gives assurance of freedom from an undeserved curse.

"An undeserved curse will be powerless to harm you. It may flutter over you like a bird, but it will find no place to land" (Proverbs 26:2 TPT). The Passion Bible says that some of the Hebrew manuscripts give the idea of a bird going back to its nest when a wrong curse has been spoken over you.[3] You have the authority to cause every undeserved curse sent against you to be reversed and to leave you.

Jesus paid the price for believers to be free from every curse that opposes their destiny. He hung on the Cross to grant freedom for believers. Christ redeemed us from the curse of the Law, having become a curse for us—for it is written,

CURSED IS EVERYONE WHO HANGS ON A TREE.
Galatians 3:13, NASB 1995

Jesus paid a great price for His followers to walk in freedom from curses–both personal and generational. Thank Him for what He did and receive the freedom to move forward into the destiny God planned for your life!

# DISCUSSION QUESTIONS

1. Why does the enemy want you to miss your destiny?
2. Describe spiritual warfare.

---

[3] Passion, p. 1004.

3. What are two causes of curses in a person's life or in a territory?

4. Give an example of a prayer using the Blood of Jesus to break a curse.

5. What is an undeserved curse?

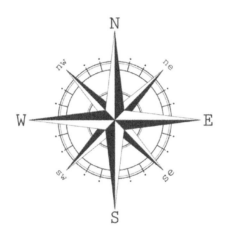

# CHAPTER 5

# Defeating Jezebel and Controlling Spirits

N ancy cried as she told me her story. She was a 45-year-old, well-educated woman. Her parents divorced when she was five years old. Nancy often wished she had other siblings, as she felt perhaps her mother would not be so possessive of her, if there were other children in the family.

Since Nancy was the only other person in her home, she did her best to make her mother happy. She ate the same food that her mother liked. She didn't invite her friends to come to her house, since she knew they were not the kind of friends her mother would think were good enough. Nancy even graduated from the same college her mother had graduated from. That made Nancy's mother very proud of her!

Later in life, Nancy and her husband moved to a different state. The pressure from her mother had become too great! The frequent phone calls and visits affected not only Nancy but affected her marriage. Surely, Nancy could break her mother's habit of calling several times each day by living about a thousand miles away.

Moving to a distant city did not stop the phone from ringing! In fact, her mother became very angry if Nancy did not return her calls several times each day! She accused Nancy of abandoning her at a time when she needed her the most. After all, she was an elderly woman. What could Nancy do? She felt trapped by a mother who was in her 80s. She felt guilty for even wishing her mother would die. Anything to stop the control!

## Controlling spirits hinder destiny.

A controlling spirit can hinder a person's destiny. Nancy could not be who God made her to be if she allowed her mother to continue controlling her life. The pain and frustration probably had to get very bad before Nancy recognized it. After all, this situation had been the same throughout Nancy's life. It may have seemed normal. One role of a mother is to help a child learn good behavior. Maybe her mother thought she was trying to help Nancy learn good behavior. Maybe not.

Part of the problem was that Nancy was no longer a child. She was an adult who needed to make her own decisions in life. Yet, the umbilical cord in the emotional realm was still attached! Nancy, like so many other people, needed to be free from a controlling spirit. Otherwise, she would never reach her God-given destiny.

Nehemiah was a man in the Old Testament who had a destiny in life to fulfill. He lived in a comfortable palace as the cupbearer to the Persian king. Nehemiah received favor from the king to go to Jerusalem and help the displaced citizens who were returning to rebuild their city.

Once the work of restoration in Jerusalem began, opposition surfaced. Enemies arose to stop Nehemiah from fulfilling the destiny God had planned for him. Sanballat and Tobiah were controllers who attempted to stop the work of rebuilding the city.

> Now it came about that when Sanballat heard that we were rebuilding the wall, he became furious and very angry and mocked the Jews. He spoke in the presence of his brothers and the wealthy *men* of Samaria and said, "What are these feeble Jews doing? Are they going to restore *it* for themselves? Can they offer sacrifices? Can they finish in a day? Can they revive the stones from the dusty rubble, even the burned ones?" Now Tobiah the Ammonite *was* near him and he said, "Even what they are building–if a fox should jump on *it*, he would break their stone wall down!"
>
> Nehemiah 4:1-3

Sanballat and Tobiah provide a picture of controlling spirits. They employed the usual tactics of control to stop Nehemiah in pursuing his God-given destiny. They used anger, mocking, intimidation, and fear. They spoke in the presence of their brothers to entice others to yield to their controlling spirits. A controlling spirit will always attempt to seduce other people to join their cause.

Nehemiah refused to be controlled by the enemy. He had a destiny to fulfill. He refused to waste time defending his actions with controlling spirits. Nehemiah prayed and continued doing the work God had assigned to him. You have a destiny to fulfill. Keep moving forward. Learn to choose your battles! Your battle is not with flesh and blood. You are dealing with a demonic spirit that is attempting to stop you in your assignment.

> Your hand-to-hand combat is not with human beings, but with the highest principalities and authorities operating in rebellion under the heavenly realms. For they are a powerful class of demon-gods and evil spirits that hold this dark world in bondage. Because of this, you must wear all the armor that God provides so you're protected as you confront the slander, for you are destined for all things and will rise victorious.
>
> Ephesians 6:12-13 TPT

However, you are not without help! The Lord made a way for His people to discern and deal with a wrong spirit of control.

## Discerning of spirits

Not every manifestation of control is a demon. Sometimes a person controls because of religious beliefs, emotional insecurities, fear of not being able to protect themselves, or many other issues. Some of these issues need healing.

The person may be a "born-again" Christian. They are trying to live a righteous life. However, the deep wounds from past trauma, neglect, abuse, rejection, and many other issues surface when the person is under stress. Transformation occurs when these deep wounds are healed. Following this healing, the actions change. Then the emotions change. A good counselor or mentor can help with the healing process.

If a wrong spirit is involved, God has made a way for believers to recognize that spirit. The Bible calls recognizing wrong spirits as the *gift of discerning of spirits*. I wrote about this gift in my book, *Removing the Veil of Deception*.

> The Holy Spirit empowers the believer with the gift of discerning of spirits. This is no mental exercise. Rather,

it is a supernatural gift given in the very moment it is needed...God has given every believer the Holy Spirit... God's Spirit is given to believers as a weapon to free them from wrong spirits. When this gift is operating, a believer can know immediately what is motivating a person or situation.[1]

## Symptoms of control

Believers can recognize a spirit of control through some of the symptoms that a controller manifests. One symptom of control is anger. The person becomes angry when things don't go the way he or she wants. No one wants to confront or disagree with that person. People become afraid of the person. They suppress any ideas of their own. They simply cower to the wishes of the controller. Anger is a weapon used to control others so that the controlling person is always right.

Another symptom of control is guilt. People who control others use guilt to get what they want. Often, you will hear a controlling person say something like this. "After all I have done for you, look at what you are doing to me." Or this, "You don't really love me, or you wouldn't be doing this." The intent is to make that person feel guilty and cause them to change what they are doing. Many people are prone to guilt and become gullible to this attack. Past wounding may cause the person to feel responsible for everything in life that goes wrong. Therefore, they can be controlled by feelings of guilt.

The controller may use both tactics as they try to control the situation. If anger doesn't work, they try guilt. That also works vice-versa. Whatever it takes, the controller relentlessly pursues control of the agenda.

---

[1] Barbara Wentroble, *Removing the Veil of Deception, How to Recognize Lying Signs, False Wonders and Seducing Spirits* (Grand Rapids, MI: Chosen Books, 2009), p. 77.

Being controlled or controlling others will hinder a person from reaching their destiny. We need the Spirit of the Lord to set us free from any of these maladies.

## Jezebel

A good picture of a controlling spirit is found in the Old Testament in 1 Kings 16:31 and 2 Kings 9, and also mentioned in the New Testament in Revelation 2:20. These scriptures describe the life of Queen Jezebel. Jezebel was the wife of King Ahab who ruled Israel. She was a rebellious, manipulative person. Jezebel was a very religious woman. In fact, she was "super-spiritual." However, her religion was a false religion that included witchcraft and harlotries. She had her own false prophets and hated the true prophets of God.

The Bible gives the picture of a female Jezebel. Understand, however, that a Jezebel *spirit* is neither male nor female. Because of that, this spirit can operate through any gender. Anyone can succumb to that evil spirit.

The main characteristic of a controlling spirit, a Jezebel spirit, is manipulation. Manipulation is when the controller, operating out of a Jezebel spirit, exerts calculated and cunning influence over another person's mind and emotions to do what *they* want, even if the person would not normally do that particular thing. If the person being manipulated eventually discerns the tactics of the controller, they may attempt to stop doing what the controller wants. When this happens, the controller may act angry, verbalize threats, or abruptly cease the relationship with the person, even influencing others to reject and isolate the person. The controller will do whatever it takes to get people to do the things he or she wants.

The Jezebel spirit uses its influence and religious gifting to bring division in personal relationships, communities, churches, organizations, etc. Jezebel will not stay in a *close* relationship unless it can *control* the relationship. The primary motive of division is to get rid of anyone who may actually discern that spirit in operation and expose them.

The controlling person often brings division by spreading gossip about the person that will not come under its control. Being religious, the controller often shares accusing dreams or visions they had about the person they can't control. Since the root of control is fear, the fearful controller must do whatever is necessary to be in control of people or situations. Jezebel seduces people to come alongside her and her ungodly schemes. Her desire is to lead God's people away from their first love, the Lord Jesus. She wants to be first in their lives! Her seduction can continue until she leads people into idolatry and sexual immorality. The Book of Revelation warns the church against the seducing power of Jezebel.

> I have *this* against you, that you tolerate the woman Jezebel, who calls herself a prophetess, and she teaches and leads My bondservants astray, so that they commit *acts of* immorality and eat things sacrificed to idols.
>
> Revelation 2:20

Francis Frangipane, a Christian evangelical minister and author, says the name Jezebel literally means "without cohabitation." He goes on to say the controller will not cohabit with any person that he cannot control.[2]

Jezebel is often found in a position of leadership like Queen Jezebel. The person may not always be in leadership but attempts to influence leadership. This spirit manifests as very religious, strong-willed, and generally operates through an extraordinarily gifted person. This spirit is like a spiritual cancer. It is opposed to a new move of God. It uses its power to keep people from stepping into their true identity and fulfilling their God-given destiny.

---

[2] Francis Frangipane, *The Jezebel Spirit* (Cedar Rapids, IA: Advancing Church Ministries, 1991), p. 2.

The story of Jezebel in 1 Kings 18 is a good example of the power of God's Spirit versus demonic power. The prophets of Baal were controlled by Jezebel. These false prophets engaged in a spiritual challenge against Elijah, a true prophet of God. The false prophets built an altar and drenched it with water. They prayed and called out to Baal to bring fire down on the water-soaked sacrifices. The prayers became desperate as the false prophets prayed hour after hour. Still, no fire came down.

Finally, Elijah called out to the God of Abraham, Isaac and Israel. He asked the Lord to answer him and let the people know He is the true God. When Elijah prayed, God answered by fire!

> Then the fire of the Lord fell, and consumed the burnt offering and the wood and the stones and the dust, and licked up the water that was in the trench. And when all the people saw it, they fell on their faces; and they said, "The Lord, He is God; the Lord, He is God."
>
> 1 Kings 18:38-39

God's power was greater than the power of the false prophets of Baal. God's power was greater than the power of Jezebel that controlled them!

**Witchcraft control**

A witchcraft spirit can be motivating the controlling person. Witchcraft is a demonic spirit that is often used by a strong controller. The controller usually seems to be very religious. Remember, Jezebel had prophets–although false ones! Often religious control is used to stop a person from fulfilling their destiny. Scriptures are often quoted to get the person to do the bidding of the controller. "Do not touch My anointed ones, and do My prophets no harm" (1 Chronicles 16:22).

The controller comes across as so super-spiritual that no one else around them thinks they can ever get into such a high calling of God. The controlled person feels ignorant and incapable of making right decisions. They feel trapped in their circumstances. They eventually believe they are immature and need the controller in their lives.

Jennifer LeClaire exposes the tactics of a Jezebel spirit that uses witchcraft in her book, *Satan's Deadly Trio, Defeating the Deceptions of Jezebel, Religion and Witchcraft.*

> Jezebel wants to castrate you spiritually–strip you of your power. Jezebel does this by working with religion to muddy your identity in Christ and convince you that you cannot exercise your authority in Him because you made a mistake last week. So you begin speaking death instead of life over yourself–and essentially releasing word curses against your own life. Once you are spiritually weakened, Jezebel has you right where it wants you.[3]

## Jehu spirit

Thankfully, the Holy Spirit can empower a believer to overcome the enemy's plans. God has a supernatural anointing available to all believers. Part of that anointing is the Spirit of Jehu.

Jehu was a king in Israel. He was sent by the word of Elisha to defeat the woman, Jezebel. Jehu had Jezebel killed and thrown down from her lofty position.

> He said, "Throw her down." So they threw her down, and some of her blood was sprinkled on the wall and on the horses, and he trampled her under foot.
>
> 2 Kings 9:33

We must be like Jehu. We must have a warring spirit to defeat Jezebel. Only a Jehu anointing can destroy the Jezebel spirit. We

---

[3] Jennifer LeClaire, *Satan's Deadly Trio, Defeating the Deceptions of Jezebel, Religion and Witchcraft* (Minneapolis, MN: Chosen Books, 2014), p. 57.

must not be like the church in Thyatira, a wealthy city in Asia Minor, that tolerated the woman Jezebel. (See Revelation 2:20.) Her manipulation, seduction, false prophets, and evil, controlling ways are not part of God's plan for your life. God has destined you for freedom to fulfill your purpose and reach your destiny.

## Freedom from control

If an evil spirit is causing a person to be a controller, the person needs to be set free from that wrong spirit. It is not always easy to acknowledge having a controlling spirit. Pride can keep the person from admitting their condition. Honesty and humility open the door to freedom. Once the person recognizes and admits their condition, they are on the road to recovery. God loves a humble heart.

> When you act with presumption, convinced that you're right, don't be surprised if you fall flat on your face! But walking in humility helps you to make wise decisions.
>
> Proverbs 11:2 TPT

God wants His people free from anything the enemy sends into their lives. Once the person's eyes are open to truth, the person can advance into freedom. "You shall know the truth, and the truth shall make you free" (John 8:32). The controlling person can now reject the controlling spirit operating through them and receive God's grace to walk in the freedom of the Lord.

If you sense that you are a person with a controlling spirit, you may want to pray this prayer:

*Father, I come to you in gratitude for revealing to me that I have a controlling spirit. I confess that I was blind, but now I see. Forgive me for allowing that spirit to operate through me. I ask for forgiveness for those that I harmed through my wrong behavior. Cleanse me from all unrighteousness. I reject any controlling spirit*

*in my life! I command it to leave me now! I receive the grace to walk
with a humble heart. Thank you, Lord, for setting me free!*

A person being controlled by others can do the same thing. The
person being controlled can forgive the controller, reject the
spirit of control, and receive the grace of God to walk free. If
you are being controlled, you may want to pray a prayer like this:

*Father, thank You that You have a hope and a future for me. You
will make a way for my purpose and my destiny to be realized. I
confess that I have allowed a controlling spirit to hinder my destiny.
I forgive the person that has controlled my life and my decisions. I
ask you to heal them from their own hurts. Deliver them from a
wrong spirit. I repent for allowing my life to be led by control rather
than being led by your Spirit. I reject any controlling spirit over my
life. I command it to be broken off my life now! I receive God's grace
to move forward in freedom. I choose to be guided by the Holy
Spirit. Thank you, Lord, for setting me free!*

## DISCUSSION QUESTIONS

1. Discuss any encounter you have experienced with a
   controlling spirit.
2. What are several symptoms of a controlling spirit?
3. Describe Jezebel found in the Old Testament.
4. How is Jezebel connected to religion?
5. Define a Jehu spirit.

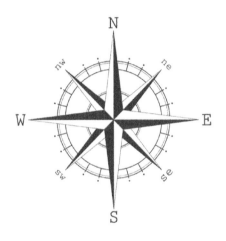

# CHAPTER 6

# Dreams and Visions That Reveal Your Destiny

S ome people are amazing overcomers! Each time a situation in life tries to knock them down, they get up and go again. My friend Mona is like that. She has been through many battles. However, as she wars through each battle, she becomes stronger and continues to press into her God-given destiny!

A recent note from Mona helped me understand how she can rise above every opposing force sent against her. She wrote how a dream confirmed her commitment to fulfilling God's purpose for her life. Here is her dream.

Jesus came to me, but I did not see His face. He gently took my hand, and we began to walk. We walked down an amazing path that had fruit that was lasting fruit. The fruit was so large that it hung to the ground. Flowers along the path were large and beautiful.

Jesus then spoke to me, "Ramona (my real name), you know that you chose this path." I asked Him what that meant. Jesus said, "Before you were born you said 'Yes' to your life. All that you have been through, the suffering, the pain, the loss, the joy, Me, you chose before you ever went to Earth." He recalled to my mind several times when I said 'yes' to the Lord. "You said 'yes' in eternity past, you are saying 'yes' in eternity present, and you will say 'yes' in eternity future."

We continued to walk and came to a particularly beautiful garden. Jesus continued talking to me. "This is where your children were missing, and you chose not to turn your back on Me. You chose to say 'yes.'"

We walked and came to another garden. Jesus continued speaking to me. "This is where fear engulfed you as you were told a contract had been put on your life. Once again, you said 'yes.'"

We came to another garden and the Lord reminded me about the 587 days of intravenous injections when I had cancer. He reminded me of another time when I had a stroke. On and on we walked. With each encounter, Jesus reminded me that I had said "yes" in eternity past.

Then Jesus began speaking softly to me. "Except a seed fall into the ground and die, it bears no fruit (John 12:24). Look around you at the times the seeds I gave you have fallen into the ground. See how I have watered them with your tears. The cry of your heart has been to have remaining fruit. It is all for eternity, Ramona."

We walked up to a gate. He put his hand on top of mine. I felt His love, passion, and His foreknowledge of what I had gone through in the past, and what I would go through in the future. How I wanted to go through the gate to the beautiful house on the other side! Jesus said, "It's yours!"

He then took my hand off the gate and said, "Not yet." I knew that I was going to make it through anything I had to walk through in life. The dream was God's way of communicating that He will give me grace and strength for the days ahead. I can make it since I said "yes" in past eternity before I came to Earth. I can make it now by saying "yes" in eternity present. I am convinced that I will say "yes" in eternity future!

Mona said she had only four to five dreams during her life that she believes are from the Lord, and she knew this dream was a God-dream. Her husband said that, when she woke from sleep after having the dream, she glowed with the presence of the Lord!

**Why dreams and visions?**
Dreams and visions are some of the ways God communicates with His people. He promised long ago He would give His people the ability to hear His voice through dreams.

> And it will come about after this that I will pour out My Spirit on all mankind; and your sons and daughters will prophesy, your old men will dream dreams, your young men will see visions. And even on the male and female servants I will pour out My Spirit in those days.
>
> Joel 2:28-29

The Lord has guided people through nearly every turning point in history by using dreams. In Genesis 28, God gave Jacob a very vivid and memorable dream, often now referred to as "Jacob's ladder." The dream was a promise to Jacob for his destiny.

> He came to a certain place and spent the night there, because the sun had set; and he took one of the stones of the place and put it under his head, and lay down in that place. And he had a dream, and behold, a ladder was set on the earth with its top reaching to heaven; and behold, the angels of God were ascending and descending on it. And behold, the LORD stood above it and said, "I am the LORD, the God of your father Abraham and the God of Isaac; the land on which you lie, I will give it to you and to your descendants.
>
> Genesis 28:11-13

## Visions

Much that applies to dreams also applies to visions. The difference is the person is awake when visions occur. The Bible is filled with stories of people who received a vision from the Lord. Some of these visions brought revelation for the person to walk in God's destiny for their life. Peter's commission to eat with and minister to Gentiles came through a vision. (See Acts 10.)

A Gentile by the name of Cornelius feared God, gave alms to the Jewish people, and prayed to God. He had a vision of an angel that told him God had heard his prayers. He was told to send men to Joppa and bring back a man by the name of Peter. Cornelius sent the men on their way in obedience to the vision.

While the men were traveling, Peter went to pray up on the rooftop of the house where he was staying. While he prayed, he became hungry, fell into a trance, and then had a vision. God spoke and told him to eat animals which his Jewish religion considered unclean. The Lord continued to speak to Peter concerning his assignment. Peter was perplexed at God's instructions. At the end of the vision, he was told to follow the men who would be arriving soon.

Peter obediently followed the men to the house of Cornelius. According to the Jewish regulations, Jews were not to enter the house of any Gentile, as Gentiles were considered unclean. Regardless, and in obedience to the Lord, Peter entered Cornelius' house, and the Spirit of God fell on all those present. God demonstrated He loved and accepted both Jew and Gentile. Gentiles were now welcome to the Kingdom of God! A breakthrough by the Spirit of God occurred when Peter and Cornelius were obedient to the revelations they received through a vision. Aren't we thankful, as Gentiles, these visions created a pathway in the Spirit for all of us to be included in the family of God?

**Days of restoration**
God communicates to people today in the same way that He spoke to Jacob, Cornelius, and Peter. A prophetic dream is one of the manifestations of God's Spirit speaking to His people. Many of the manifestations of God's Spirit we read about in the Bible stopped after about 300 AD. The Church operated in legalism and man-made traditions. They embraced many pagan practices and, therefore, did not possess God's Holy Spirit. God did not move away from His people. God's people moved away from Him; however, God was not finished speaking to His people. Restoration of truths found in the Bible are progressively being restored. We are now in those days of restoration.

Restoration began in the early 1500s with a German monk named Martin Luther. He taught salvation and eternal life are not earned by good works. He saw in Scripture it is by faith and not by works people are justified and saved. That was revelation during his time! Legalism and religious works were rampant in the Church. With Luther's revelation, believers once again could experience new life through the power of the Holy Spirit.

From the time of Martin Luther, God has been restoring truth found in the Bible. Part of the restoration is the supernatural manifestations of God's Spirit. Spiritual dreams and visions are supernatural. They are sometimes used to help believers on the path to their destiny.

**Interpreting dreams and visions**
Dream interpretation is the function of a prophetic anointing. Not everyone is a prophet. Yet, the Bible says all can prophesy. (See 1 Corinthians 14:31.) A person does not need to be a prophet to interpret dreams. However, a strong prophetic gift usually allows the person to interpret dreams in a greater way.

Prophetic dreams and visions are linked to the seer gift. Jim Goll describes the operation of the seer gift in his book, *The Seer, The Prophetic Power of Visions, Dreams, and Open Heavens.*

> The seer realm describes a whole other aspect of the way the prophetic operation occurs. Generally speaking, seers are people who see visions in a consistent and regular manner. For the most part, their prophetic anointing is more *visionary* than auditory. Rather than receiving words that they attempt to repeat or flow with, they often see pictures that they then describe. These pictures may be in the form of waking visions, or as dreams while sleeping.[1]

A lot of symbolism is used in dreams and visions. People, places, and things often represent something other than what the person sees. In particular, it is important for a person to have a right interpretation of a negative dream before sharing it with others. For example, there have been times when a person has shared publicly about a minister or leader they dreamed about. Sometimes in the dream, they saw the person committing a

---

[1] Jim W. Goll, *The Seer, The Prophetic Power of Visions, Dreams, and Open Heavens* (Shippensburg, PA: Destiny Image Publishers, Inc., 2004), p. 23.

sexual sin. That does not mean that the person they saw in the dream was committing a sexual sin. The leader in the dream could represent another person, an evil spirit, or even their own need for healing. Sharing a dream like that without proper interpretation has caused much hurt, confusion, and division in the Church.

**Scriptural foundation**

A good scriptural foundation is *vital* for dream interpretation. God will never speak contrary to His Word. Too often, people rush to tell others, without any biblical or prayerful consideration, what God spoke to them through a dream or vision. Often, what the person heard is not consistent with scripture.

I remember a man many years ago who shared what he felt God had said to him. He was married, and the couple led a vibrant, growing Christian youth program. He said God told him to leave his wife and marry another woman. The other woman was married at the time. Both the man and the married woman left their spouses. They moved in together but never got married. The youth group broke up and no longer existed. The man went from one relationship to another through the years. He followed a soulish desire rather than the Lord. God would never tell someone to leave their spouse and destroy another marriage. How vital it is to have a strong biblical foundation for direction toward a person's God-given destiny!

I love the way Jane Hamon cautions believers when interpreting spiritual dreams or visions.

We should never depend solely upon any of these prophetic means to lead us in our daily walk, although at times God may choose to speak a rhema word to us and direct us through them. We are to be led by the Spirit of God through personal prayer and the study of His Word, not by continuous dream interpretation or even prophecy. It is only as we daily follow Jesus Christ and sound Scriptural doctrine from His Word that we will receive true revelation and true interpretation of spiritual dreams and visions when they come.[2]

I occasionally have dreams that I believe are from the Lord. Most of my dreams are a result of my busy lifestyle. However, I seem to have a lot of dreams about catching an airplane. The airplane is a vehicle that gets you to a place you need to be. These airplanes in my dreams seem to indicate the pursuit of my destiny in life, and I am always attempting to get where I need to be. I am moving forward in my purpose to reach my destiny. We don't always need to know the exact destiny God has for us. We merely need to keep moving forward with Him. He sometimes sends messages to us through dreams and visions as we are pursuing our purpose with Him.

Dreams and visions are two of the ways God directs our steps. The Bible tells us God has a purpose for our lives. He also has a *time* for us to pursue the purpose He has for us.

> To everything *there* is a season, A time for every purpose under heaven.
> Ecclesiastes 3:1 NKJV

God's timing is perfect. Trust Him to lead you where you need to be. You are living in God's appointed time to walk in your destiny. Keep moving forward with the Lord! He will speak to you and direct your path into your full purpose and destiny in life!

---

[2] Jane Hamon, *Dreams and Visions* (Santa Rosa Beach, FL: Christian International Ministries, 1997), pp. 43-44.

# DISCUSSION QUESTIONS

1. What is the difference between a dream and a vision?
2. Describe a dream that you know was from the Lord.
3. Describe a vision that helped you understand a situation.
4. What is the difference between a prophet and a seer?
5. Why is it necessary to have a biblical foundation when interpreting dreams and visions?

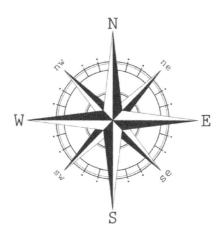

# CHAPTER 7

## Convergence of Your Past and Future to Fulfill Your Destiny

I sensed my dream was from the Lord. Not all dreams automatically mean that God is speaking to us. Some dreams occur as a result of our own emotions or circumstances we are wrestling with inside. Still, God does speak to His people through dreams. I knew this dream was one of those times.

In the dream I stood looking at a swinging bridge. I knew it was time to cross over to the other side. My destiny was not on this side of the bridge, but it was on the other side. I looked down at the boards extending along the bridge where I needed to step to cross over. Interestingly, a name was written on each board! Some of the names on the boards were *fear, wrong relationships, finances, doubts, old mindsets.* There were many boards with lots of names that I had to step on to cross over.

I knew I needed to be willing to put each of the boards, and the issues they represented, under my feet. These names were the hindrances that would stop me from reaching my future destiny. They were designed to keep me in an old place. I had the choice to stay on this side of the bridge if I would not be willing to address each hindrance.

Looped along each side of the bridge were ropes to hold onto. If I didn't hold on to the ropes, I could easily fall off the bridge. Looking down, all I could see was a dark, dry trench with no water in it. I suddenly realized these ropes were Ropes of Hope! Jesus is our Hope. I had to hold onto Him to cross over into my future.

Somehow the Lord gave me the courage and boldness to step on the boards. The Bible tells us wherever we have put our feet, we possess that land. (See Deuteronomy 11:24.) I was now on the way to my destiny. I sensed the Lord empowered me to create a convergence of my past on the old side of the bridge to my future on the other side of the bridge. I could then reach the destiny God had prepared for my life.

## Convergence

There is a time when our destiny involves the coming together of our past and our future. Convergence is the act of coming together. Our past experiences, skills, dreams, and many other factors come together to shape our future. Old mindsets must change for this to happen. Often, relationships change, jobs change, finances change, and there may be many other lifestyle changes. A person begins to realize their true identity changes from who they thought they were to who they really are!

## Reinvent

Often, an individual reaches a time in life, usually around 40-50 years old, when they realize that they cannot do in the future what they did in the past. That individual must reinvent themself for the new season. To reinvent themself, a person discovers again what is their destiny in life. They may have thought their destiny was in one direction. Now, they think again and realize God has something different for their future.

I once heard a report that culture reinvents itself every five years. It seems to happen much more frequently than that today! Yet, the Church usually reinvents itself every 50 years! I wonder, is that the reason why many people feel the Church is irrelevant in today's culture? We all may have experienced times in our life when we were faced with the decision to reinvent ourselves, our ministry, or our business – or all three! – in order to stay relevant in today's world and culture.

## Your core

When a person reinvents themself for the new season, their function may change. For instance, a doctor may have had a family practice in the last season. As the doctor converges in the new season, he may volunteer for a humanitarian project. While serving in that project, the doctor may use some of his medical skills from the past season. Those skills converge with a desire to help on mission projects in underdeveloped nations. The doctor finds himself doing what has been in his heart for many years.

Very important to note here, when the function changes, the core should *not* change. Your core is who you *really* are. It is what you are willing to die for. More than that, it is what you are willing to *live* for! Your core is the thing that causes you to get out of bed in the morning. It is the thing that keeps you dreaming when others are caught in mediocrity. It is what you want your life to be remembered for!

After Pentecost, the Apostle Peter could not be who he was in the past season. In the past, he denied Jesus and made wrong statements. After Pentecost, he boldly confessed Jesus and preached a powerful sermon that caused 3,000 souls to come into the Kingdom in one day. Peter's function changed, but his core remained the same. His core caused him to live a life of obedience to the calling of God on his life. The Bible does not tell us how Peter died. However, tradition says he was hung upside down in Rome. There is no proof of this, but at that time, it appears as though he was martyred. Obviously, by reinventing himself, Apostle Peter was not only willing to live for the cause of Christ but was also willing to die for it. His core never changed!

**Repackage for your future**

Not only do we need to reinvent ourselves for the new season, but we also may need to repackage our life. Repackaging our life can propel us into the amazing destiny that God has for us.

I watched a movie several years ago, which, for me, is a rare occasion. In the movie, the lead character had to repackage what he had from the past and give it a new look for the future. He was a toy manufacturer. Old toys lined the shelves of his company. No one wanted the old toys, since they preferred the new ones. The man was facing bankruptcy when an angel, in the guise of a short man, showed up at his business. The angel helped the business owner develop a new strategy. He showed the business owner how to take what he already had in his hands and repackage it for the future.

The store workers would repackage the old toys with a new look. Old toys were put in a box, and the box was marked as a Surprise Box. Buyers did not know what was in the boxes. They were surprised after opening the box to find old, outdated toys. The buyers loved it! The strategy was a huge success! The business owner already had in his hands what it would take to break out of the old place and converge into his future. He merely had to repackage what he had from the past and give it a new look for his future.

## What is in your hands?

I remember a time when I was struggling to find a way to do what I felt the Lord wanted me to do. I needed a place to hold meetings to equip believers for Kingdom purposes. I looked at rental property. I looked at finances. The task seemed impossible. The cost for rental property and available finances certainly did not converge!

As I pondered my situation, I sensed a powerful question from the Lord. "Barbara, what do you have in your hands?" Suddenly, I looked around. I had office space that could be rearranged. Chairs could be purchased locally at a reasonable price. I had in my hands everything necessary to move into the new season. I could repackage what I already had and give a new look to what I was called to do. Converging my past ministry experience with the new Kingdom venture would put me on the path to my destiny!

## Convergence of Moses' life

Many biblical characters had to converge their past experiences to their future destiny. Moses did that. He knew that God had a future and purpose for his life. In the old season, Moses attempted to fulfill his destiny as a deliverer by killing an Egyptian. He spent the next 40 years in a desert with pressure that would prepare him for his destiny.

The time came for a convergence of Moses' past to his future. He noticed a burning bush that was not consumed. As he turned aside to see the unusual bush, the Lord's voice apprehended him. God talked with Moses about his destiny as a deliverer of God's people.

As Moses made excuses about why he could not do what God was asking him to do, God replied with a question. "What do you have in your hands?" Moses responded to the Lord's command to throw the stick in his hand to the ground. The staff became a snake. When Moses picked it up, the snake became a staff. God revealed to Moses that He was going to take his staff from the past season and repackage it with supernatural power. Moses would use it to fulfill his destiny as a deliverer of God's people. He could not deliver the Israelites from Egypt 40 years before. Now, the time had arrived for a convergence from being a mere shepherd in the desert to reinventing himself as God's ambassador to free an entire nation! What he could not do in the past season, he was now equipped with supernatural tools to fulfill his destiny!

## Convergence for such a time as this

The story of Esther in the Bible encourages even the most hopeless people about their future. Esther was an orphan. She may not have had the right education, the right family background, the finances, or many other things that most people sense are necessary for fulfilling their destiny. None of these circumstances hinder God's plan for His people.

God had a plan for Esther's destiny in the same way that He has a plan for your destiny. Circumstances do not limit the power of God to take situations from the past and cause them to converge with your future destiny.

Before God could deliver her nation, God had to deliver Esther from her past limitations. In the natural, she seemed like the least likely person to be used by God. Esther needed to reinvent herself from the identity as an orphan to the identity of a queen. She had to repackage herself to step into her destiny. Repackaging would give her a new look. Her past was not her future! She was not born to be an orphan, but she was born to be a queen.

To reach her God-given destiny, Esther spent a year being repackaged for her future. Old garments had to be discarded. A new fragrance had to cover her. The focus was not on her past. The focus had to be on preparation for her future.

Once Esther became queen, she did not live in a soft, cozy environment. Becoming queen was only part of the process to get her to the destiny God planned for her life. The pressure of her repackaging was not an easy task. Repackaging for destiny can be a stressful process. She understood the pressure of the strategic times she lived in. The past identity as an orphan was gasping for breath to live again. The future identity and destiny for Esther as a queen was kicking hard to be born. The stress and pressure of her repackaging would now give her the courage she needed to fulfill her assignment from the Lord.

Like Esther of old, we have come into the Kingdom "for such a time as this" (Esther 4:14). Believers must press through the difficulty of letting go of the old season. God's intent is not to take us *out* of the pressure but to bring us *through* the pressure. Like the repackaging of the caterpillar that becomes a butterfly, we are being squeezed into our future.

**Convergence is a journey.**
Convergence doesn't happen overnight. It is often a process. Moses didn't deliver the Israelites overnight. Esther didn't save her nation overnight. You and I face the same obstacles. We are on a journey into our future. Learning to navigate the path in front of us takes time. Realizing that we already have in our hands the necessary tool for our future inspires us to keep moving forward.

The temptation a person faces is the desire to return to the old place while transitioning to convergence. Even though we may not have enjoyed some of the situations in the past, we tend to only remember the good things. The Israelites remembered the food, safe homes, and provision, however meager, they had in Egypt. They tended to forget the slavery, hardness of hearts in their taskmasters, and the captivity of their lives. There was a desire for the comforts and familiarity of the past.

Captivity limited the Israelites. They were limited in their knowledge and experience. It was difficult to imagine being in a place they had never experienced. During convergence, the temptation will be to go back to a familiar place. You remember what it was like doing the things you were good at doing. You remember the people's lives you touched, the financial income, and so many other things that were good. You are now entering into unfamiliar territory. Like the Apostle Paul, a person must resist the temptations to go back to an old place.

> Brethren, I do not regard myself as having laid hold of *it* yet; but one thing *I do*: forgetting what *lies* behind and reaching forward to what *lies* ahead, I press on toward the goal for the prize of the upward call of God in Christ Jesus.
> Philippians 3:13-14

You are stepping into the best time of your life. Doing what you are created to do will keep you moving forward while others retire. Your best years are not behind you. They are in front of you! You will accelerate as you reinvent yourself and repackage what you have in your hands. Enjoy the journey!

# DISCUSSION QUESTIONS

1. What is convergence?
2. What part of your life do you need to reinvent?
3. Describe your core that you need to take with you during convergence.
4. What do you have in your hands that will be useful as you experience convergence?
5. What is the greatest temptation you face as you walk into convergence?

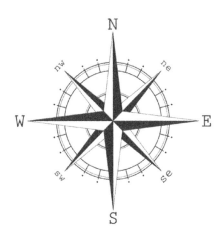

# CHAPTER 8

# Relationships That Shape
# Your Destiny

D
ale and I had been through a very difficult season! Friends left us. People we had poured our hearts and lives into turned against us. It was a very painful and confusing time. After a couple of years, a door opened for a new job for Dale. The job would require us to move from East Texas to Dallas. I had felt a strong word from the Lord two years prior that we would be moving to Dallas. So, the decision was an easy

decision. We didn't know anyone in the Dallas area, and I did not minister in that city. Yet, I had a visitation from the Lord. In that special encounter with the Lord, He promised favor and advancement, as He transitioned us to a new place.

After moving to the Dallas area, we found ourselves in a very loving, friendly church. The teachings and ministry were so powerful! We thought we had arrived in Heaven! Along with a wonderful spiritual atmosphere was the connection with Apostle Jim and Jean Hodges. Somehow, they saw in us what we did not see in ourselves. Apostle Jim kept reaching out to us to schedule dinner with them. I thought he was simply being nice. He couldn't possibly want to have dinner with *us*! However, he continued inviting us to dinner until I finally said, "Yes."

That began a relationship that forever changed our lives! Jim and Jean loved us into healing. They were not interested in anything or anybody from our past. They were simply interested in being part of our lives. They were interested in our vision for the future. How refreshing!

Our friendship with the Hodges developed into a covenant relationship and remains that way today. I often tell them, "You can't get rid of us!" The strong relationship with that couple helped shape the God-given destiny for Dale and me. I often wonder, where would we be today if the Hodges had not reached out to a broken, disheartened couple? Good relationships in life can heal and restore a person. Those relationships will propel a person into the destiny God planned for their life.

**Not good to be alone**
The Lord knew that people needed others in life to reach their destiny. They needed relationships to find fulfillment in life. When God created Adam, He made a powerful statement. "It is not good for the man to be alone; I will make him a helper suitable for him" (Genesis 2:18). God had created all the animals and birds, and Adam observed how they each had a partner. Adam saw something else that really got his attention. Adam's

eyes were opened as he realized that he did not have a helper suitable for himself! For Adam to manage Earth, to be fruitful and multiply, Adam needed help. He needed someone like himself. None of the animals or birds were of the same nature and didn't provide a counterpart to Adam.

God knew what Adam needed and, therefore, created a helper for him. The word *help* does not infer an inferior position. The same Hebrew word for *help* is used many times in the Old Testament. One of those instances is Psalm 121:2, "My help comes from the Lord, Who made heaven and earth." God is mentioned as a divine help. He is certainly not inferior! I talk about this in my book, *Rise to Your Destiny, Woman of God.*

God always intended for men and women to walk together in partnership and fulfill His purpose in the earth. The Bible teaches that both men and women were created in God's image. They both have a direct relationship with God. Both are to share the responsibilities of bearing and rearing children and having dominion over the created order.

Women were designed by God to be helpers to men. Often, this word is interpreted to mean that women are inferior to men and are to be in a subservient position. However, the word "helper" in Hebrew is the word *ezer.* Strong's Concordance says that the word means "to protect or to aid...succor."[1] This is the same word that is used many times in Scripture to describe God as our helper. Since we know that God is not inferior or subservient to men and that women as well as men were made in God's image, we know that women are not inferior or subservient to men. Women were created as

---

[1] James Strong, *The Exhaustive Concordance of the Bible, Hebrew and Chaldee Dictionary* (McLean, VA: MacDonald Publishing Company, n.d.) Hebrew #5828.

equals with men, sharing in the assignment of ruling and having dominion in the earth.[2]

## Relationship in marriage

A man and woman's marriage relationship is a picture of Jesus and the Church.

> For this cause a man shall leave his father and mother, and shall cleave to his wife; and the two shall become one flesh. This mystery is great; but I am speaking with reference to Christ and the church.
>
> Ephesians 5:31-32

Marriage partners are called by God to walk together and fulfill His destiny for their lives. Often, a man and woman in marriage have different personalities and different abilities. My husband, Dale, and I are totally different people. It is amazing how God seems to put opposites together in marriage. Maybe He does it for a purpose. After all, in the act of creation, God took part of man and made woman.

In the beginning there was only man, and then Woman was created from one side of man. When God took part of man and created Woman, a part of man was then missing. She was taken out of the part of man close to his heart. The woman became Adam's counterpart. Adam could now make a decree with worship in his heart, as he looked at God's amazing gift to him. Women are the most beautiful in creation. What was missing from Adam became the most valuable.

---

[2] Barbara Wentroble, *Rise to Your Destiny, Woman of God* (Ventura, CA: Regal Books, 2006), p. 65.

The man said, "This is now bone of my bones,
And flesh of my flesh; She shall be called
Woman, Because she was taken out of Man."

Genesis 2:23

The two together would now begin a covenant marriage relationship. Marriage cannot be based on feelings. It must be based on commitment to the relationship. To be successful in our commitment to God, we must be faithful in our commitment to the marriage.

Out of that marriage would be multiplication as a family. The family is designed to be a representation of God's family on Earth. The Lord's plan is that His covenant be extended from marriage through the generations. Parents are to nurture and raise up godly children. God's covenant was to be taught to the succeeding generations in order that His blessings could be released on Earth. The marriage relationship was designed to propel Adam, Woman, and their offspring into their destiny!

**Detrimental relationships**

Not all relationships are good relationships. Some can even be detrimental. Those relationships require constant maintenance. Relationships like that can drain a person of energy and time. There is a lot of drama involved! Working through constant disagreements, we find ourselves unable to focus on anything else. The situation can seem like an entangled web that is almost impossible to untangle.

Too many times Christians believe that they are supposed to be friends with everyone. Some people are not looking for relationship. They are looking for someone who will allow them to continue in their selfish, sickly ways. Some relationships are poisonous. We must be able to discern the poisonous relationships! Relationships can propel us into our destiny, or they can keep us from it.

Jesus did not develop strong relationships with everyone. He was able to discern the hearts of men. He knew the ones who were able to develop meaningful relationships with Him, and those who were not.

> Jesus did not yet entrust himself to them, because he knew how fickle human hearts can be. He didn't need anyone to tell him about human nature, *for he fully understood what man was capable of doing.*
>
> John 2:24-25 TPT

We need that same discernment.

**Mentoring relationships**

Covenant relationships are wonderful. God purposed for our lives to be filled with good relationships. Still, every relationship is not a covenantal bond. Some people connect only as mentors. A mentor is a person willing to share their life and experiences with another individual. Mentors in our lives are important, as no one gets into their destiny alone! It takes others to help us get where we are willing to go.

Many people think that a spiritual mentor must be a giant in the faith with lots of giftings and abilities. Not so! Anyone can mentor when they understand the Lord and have experienced His faithfulness in their life. I love what Paul D. Stanley and Robert Clinton wrote about this in their book, *Connecting, The Mentoring Relationships You Need to Succeed in Life.*

> As a follower of Christ, you can mentor others. Whatever God has given you that has enabled you to grow and deepen your relationship with Him, you can pass on to others.[3]

---

[3] Paul D. Stanley and J. Robert Clinton, *Connecting, The Mentoring Relationships You Need to Succeed in Life* (Colorado Springs, CO: Navpress, 1992), p. 29.

Throughout the Bible, we see mentors investing their lives into others. Apostle Paul was a powerful mentor to young Timothy. Paul helped him understand the importance of godly character. He reminded Timothy about his ordination and the necessity of spiritual gifts that were imparted to him.

> For this reason I remind you to kindle afresh the gift of God which is in you through the laying on of my hands.
>
> 2 Timothy 1:6

Timothy would need the boldness and fire of the Holy Spirit to address the false apostles and evildoers that would try to infiltrate the Church. Timothy was mentored by Apostle Paul so he could fulfill his God-given destiny as a servant of the Lord. A mentor can be a valuable relationship to help a person reach their own God-given destiny!

**Coaching to reach destiny**

Another relationship that is often helpful in reaching a person's destiny is that of a coach. A coach is very helpful in getting a person moving toward their destiny when they cannot get there themselves.

Some of Webster's definitions of a coach are:[4]

- *A large, covered, four-wheeled carriage used in the 16th-19th centuries, a public conveyance...*
- *A railroad passenger car, furnishing the lowest priced seating accommodations*
- *An enclosed automobile, usually a two-door sedan*
- *A private tutor, an instructor, or trainer*

---

[4] Michael Agnes, Editor in Chief, *Webster's New World College Dictionary, Fourth Edition* (New York, NY: Macmillan USA, 1999), p. 279.

Each of these types of coaches are designed to get people into their desired destination. A private tutor or trainer can help a person move forward and reach their goal in a shorter period of time.

I read some statistics a few years ago that concluded productivity is increased by 88% when training is combined with coaching. We all need training in various areas. However, when combined with coaching, the results are greatly improved!

**Coaching versus counseling**
Coaching is not therapy or counseling. Coaches do not give advice. They do not attempt to provide all the answers for a client's situation. A therapist usually looks to the past to determine the root of the problem; however, a coach focuses only on the future. The coach helps the client determine the right steps to take. Then, the person can determine a path, based on those right steps, and achieve the desired results they are looking for.

**Coaching unlocks dreams.**
Coaching provides keys that unlock people's minds, their hearts, and their dreams. Discouragement occurs when a dream remains inside. The discouragement can lead to hopelessness. After a time, the dream dies. When that happens, the future looks bleak, and a person may even quit trying.

Your destiny waits for you. Do not allow your future to continue to be only a passing thought or an unachievable dream. You are the only person that can choose to call your dream to life. Speak life into your dream and into your destiny! Call for your destiny to arise with hope for the future!

Enlist a coach to help you get from where you are to where you want to be in God's Kingdom. In the Bible, David coached 400 men who were discouraged, in debt, and discontented. (See 1 Samuel 22:1.) Coach David took these rag-tag men from being an outcast group of men to coming into their potential. These men went from a position of insignificance to a position of being significant in advancing God's purposes on the Earth. They became a Mighty Army! Their lives became significant in advancing God's Kingdom. Your life can do the same thing!

**Jesus is the model in relationships.**
Jesus is the model we follow in our relationships. He gathered around Him those who were willing to partner with Him. He poured His life into them. The world was forever changed by those who walked in relationship with Him. The same model works today. For those who walk in a covenant relationship with Jesus, they make a difference in the world. These followers of Jesus demonstrate His life in their families, their friends, and their mentoring and coaching connections. The world is a better place because of these God-breathed relationships!

# DISCUSSION QUESTIONS

1. Describe a time when a relationship brought healing into your life.
2. How did you deal with a difficult relationship?
3. How is marriage a picture of the relationship between the Lord and the Church?
4. How has a mentoring relationship helped you?
5. What is the difference between a therapist and a coach?

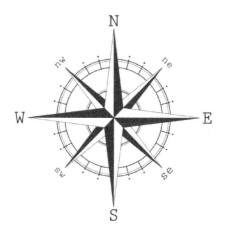

# CHAPTER 9

# Chosen in the Furnace of Affliction

I love reading stories about men and women who have impacted the world through their faith. Smith Wigglesworth is one of those people. He was a British evangelist who was very influential in the early history of the Pentecostal revival. Wigglesworth was an Apostle of faith and a pioneer in the early 1900s.

Wigglesworth was born into a very poor family. He began working in the fields with his father at age six. Due to the necessity of working at an early age, Wigglesworth was not able to read. Later, he became a plumber and was a hard worker.

After the marriage to his wife, Polly Featherstone, he functioned as an intercessor and worked to provide finances for the family. She was a preacher, and together they established a mission. After Wigglesworth was baptized in the Holy Spirit, he learned to read and became a powerful preacher. Many miracles are recorded about his ministry. History even reports dozens of people being raised from the dead. He is remembered as the "Apostle of Faith."

## Challenges to reach destiny

Difficulties in life, physical disabilities, and economic challenges did not stop Smith Wigglesworth from fulfilling his God-ordained destiny! He knew God had called him to heal the sick and perform signs and wonders as a testimony to the power of the Holy Spirit.

Wigglesworth's early life could be described as a furnace of affliction. At age six, he worked pulling turnips in the fields alongside his mother. A few years later, he worked in factories. The necessity for him to earn income to support his family created challenges in his life. His inability to read left him with many disadvantages.[1]

Rather than becoming bitter, Wigglesworth chose to allow those circumstances to make him better. With the help of the Lord, he knew he could conquer any difficult place in life. He would extinguish every fiery furnace of affliction with the fire of God's presence!

Numerous books have been written about this great man of faith. His quotes encourage readers today who seem to be living in a furnace of affliction. This is one of his quotes:

---

[1] https://en.wikipedia.org/wiki/Smith_Wigglesworth#Early_life

Great faith is the product of great fights. Great testimonies are the outcome of great tests. Great triumphs can only come out of great trials.[2]

## Destiny tested by the Lord

I have met many people who received a prophetic word about their destiny. Yet, in a short time, circumstances challenged the fulfillment of the word. People often share the same story about what happened after receiving their prophetic promise. Situations occurred that seemed to invalidate the word. Sometimes people who had been faithful in the past abandoned the promise. Finances deteriorated. Sickness occurred. Unusual spiritual attacks occurred. The person finally asks himself, *What is going on?* The prophetic word was powerful. The person felt the word was from the Lord. Yet, questions flood the person's mind concerning the fulfillment of the prophetic promise.

- *Did God really make a promise to me?*
- *Was the word from a true prophet of the Lord?*
- *Did I do something to cause the word to be invalid?*

Sometimes a person may not understand the testing that comes before reaching their destiny. Two sources of testing come in our lives. One test comes from God. His purpose is always to reveal the gold inside us. We sometimes call this the refiner's fire.

> Who can endure the day of His coming? And who can stand when He appears? For He is like a refiner's fire and like fullers'[3] soap. And He will sit as a smelter and purifier of silver, and He will purify the sons of Levi and refine them like gold

---

[2] https://www.goodreads.com/author/quotes/191049.Smith_Wigglesworth

[3] An Ancient Technique, according to Easton's Bible Dictionary, fulling is the ancient art of pressing or scouring cloth in a mill. Fullers also used their feet to stomp out garments (classroom.synonym.com).

and silver, so that they may present to the Lord offerings in righteousness.

Malachi 3:2-3

We are the temple of the Holy Spirit. God desires to cleanse us from anything that would defile us. He uses these tests to remove any bitterness, anger, or covetousness. His fire is used not only to expose our weaknesses, but also to cause us to turn to Him for help. God's fire is never to destroy us but to restore us. The refining fire is bringing us back into the image of Himself.

Throughout the Bible are stories of people having their destiny tested. Joseph was one of those people. He had a dream from the Lord as a teenager. In the dream he saw his family bowing down to him. His father even gave him a coat of many colors. The coat was a symbol of favor. Neither of those occurrences was good news to his brothers! They hated him and became jealous. Not everyone is as excited about your destiny as you are!

Roused with anger, the brothers banded together and threw Joseph into a pit. Later, they pulled him from the pit and sold him to a caravan of Ishmaelites. (See Genesis 37:28.) Once the caravan arrived in Egypt, the Ishmaelites sold Joseph as a slave. Joseph went through testing on his way to Egypt as a prisoner. How could he ever fulfill the destiny he remembered in his dream from so long ago? But God!

Different translations of the Bible describe the purpose of this season in Joseph's life.

> Until the time that his word came to pass, the word of the Lord tested him.
>
> Psalm 105:19 NASB

> God's promise to Joseph purged his character until it was time for his dreams to come true.
>
> Psalm 105:19 TPT

One of the words for "testing" in the Bible is the Greek word *dokimion.* "Knowing that the *testing* of your faith produces endurance" (James 1:3, emphasis added). Zodhiates, a complete dictionary of the Bible, says the word "dokimion" is the "means of proving, a criterion, test, by which anything is proved or tried, as faith by afflictions." The Lord uses tests to prove the good, or gold, that is in us. He does not use tests to disapprove or destroy us.[4]

## Destiny tested by the enemy

Although a person's destiny is tested by God to prove the good inside a person, the enemy also tests a person's destiny. The purpose of these tests of the enemy is to stop a person from reaching their destiny. In James 1:2, 12-14 we find the word "trial," which is also used as a *means* of testing.

"Consider it all joy, my brethren, when you encounter various *trials"* (James 1:2, emphasis added). The word "trial" in the Greek language is "peirasmos," and the root word means experience. Therefore, interpreting the meaning of the word "peirasmos" depends on *who* is doing the testing. If it is God, the means of testing, or trial, is for the purpose of proving someone and never for the purpose of causing one to fall. If the means of testing is from the enemy, the trial is expressly for the purpose of causing one to fall.[5]

In James 1:13, we find the word "tempt." In the Greek language the word is "peirazo." It is a word that means to tempt or prove by soliciting to sin. The difference between *dokimazo* (testing) and *peirazo* (tempted) is that the latter has the intention of proving that one has been evil or to make him evil. In contrast, the intent of *dokimazo* is to prove someone good and acceptable.

---

[4] Spiros Zodhiates, *The Hebrew Greek Key Study Bible, New American Standard, Lexical Aids to the New Testament* (La Habra, CA: AMG Publishers, 1990), p. 1826.

[5] Ibid, p. 1866.

Satan tempts (peirazo) to show someone unapproved. Satan is even called *pierastes*, the tempter.[6]

Several examples of the word "peirazo" are in the Bible. (See Matthew 22:18, 35, and 1 Thessalonians 3:5.) One example is when the Pharisees and Sadducees were trying to prove Jesus as evil. "The Pharisees and Sadducees came up, and testing Him asked Him to show them a sign from Heaven" (Matthew 16:1). The religious leaders constantly tested Jesus to try to entice Him to sin or find evil in Him. None of their testing succeeded. Jesus was without sin and perfect in His ways.

**Fiery furnace of testing**
Often, we are tempted to think God has changed His mind about our destiny, particularly when we are in the midst of difficulties. Sometimes we think the prophetic word we received was a false prophecy. It is then we must allow the Lord to bring us through the testing of our destiny. Often, He is doing things we do not see. A greater level of anointing and authority is waiting for those who come through the fiery furnace of testing.

A picture of the fiery furnace of testing is found in the Book of Daniel. Three men, Shadrach, Meshach, and Abednego, were ordered to be thrown into a flaming furnace, because they would not worship any god but the true God. King Nebuchadnezzar ordered the furnace to be heated seven times hotter than usual. The three men made a declaration that their God was able to deliver them from the furnace. They also declared that, even if He did not, they would not serve any other god.

The three men were bound up and cast into the furnace. Later, as the king looked inside, he saw a sight that caused him to issue a decree against anyone who spoke against the true God.

---

[6] Ibid.

94

> Then Nebuchadnezzar the king was astounded and stood up in haste; he responded and said to his high officials, "Was it not three men we cast bound into the midst of the fire?" They answered and said to the king, "Certainly, O king." He answered and said, "Look! I see four men loosed and walking about in the midst of the fire without harm, and the appearance of the fourth is like a son of the gods."
>
> Daniel 3:24-25

Even though the king witnessed the three men tied up and cast into the furnace of blazing fire, he saw them now set free, loosed from their bonds, and walking around in the furnace. Miraculously, the three men were not alone in the furnace. A fourth man was walking with them. Jesus was in the furnace with the three men. Shadrach, Meshach, and Abednego came out from the furnace untouched by the fire and without the smell of smoke on them. The fire had no effect on the bodies of the men, nor was a hair on their heads singed. As a result, the king caused the three men to prosper in the province of Babylon.

As we walk through the furnace of affliction, Jesus walks with us. He only allows the furnace to burn up the things that keep us bound and prevent us from being formed into His image. We can come forth without the smell of the smoke of bitterness, anger, and self-pity. He changes the smell of the furnace to the sweet smell of the incense of a life sacrificed to Him. Only God will be blessed and glorified.

As we walk in the destiny of God, we, too, will go through the fiery furnace. We will go through the floodwaters. We will encounter the enemy who comes as a roaring lion. Yet, the Lord is always with us.

> When you pass through the waters, I will be with you; and through the rivers, they will not overflow you. When you walk through the fire,

you will not be scorched, nor will the flame burn
you.

Isaiah 43:2

Why do we go through these hard places? As we allow
God to take us through them, He reveals our true identities and
secures the promise for our destiny.

Behold, I have refined you, but not as silver; I
have tested you in the furnace of affliction.

Isaiah 48:10

In this verse, the word "tested" is *bachar* in the Hebrew language.
"Bachar" means "chosen or selected; selected from the
choicest."[7] As we go through the furnace of affliction, the Lord,
the fourth man in the furnace, walks with us. He chooses us as
selected ones from the choicest on Earth.

Not only are we refined and chosen in the furnace of
affliction, but we are also there for another purpose. The Lord
releases a greater level of authority in our lives. We go through
the furnace to teach the furnace a lesson — that we can go
through the fire and not be burned! We go through the waters
to teach the waters a lesson — that we will not drown! There is a
lion of the tribe of Judah, and He has prevailed! (See Revelation
5:5.)

Don't quit in the midst of your fiery furnace. Your true
identity as God's choicest one is being revealed. Your destiny
awaits. You were born for this moment in time!

---

[7] Logos Library System, *New American Standard Bible Greek Dictionary*,
updated ed. (La Habra, CA: Lockman Foundation, 1995), p. 977.

# DISCUSSION QUESTIONS

1. What is one of the challenges you are facing in pursuit of your destiny?
2. Describe the questions you have while pursuing your destiny.
3. What is God's purpose in allowing testing in your life?
4. Does God use the service of Satan to subject man to trials?
5. How has a prophetic word been tested in your life?
6. What are some of the lessons learned in the furnace of affliction?

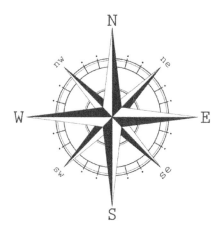

# CHAPTER 10

# Spiritual Alignment for Your Life's Assignment

Major leaders gathered from many nations around the world. The purpose of the conference was the opportunity to meet other leaders and share information about the present move of God. Discussions were held on current topics in which the leaders were involved. The topic for the panel that I was leading was *Apostolic Covering*.

The panel discussion was lively! Several leaders expressed their personal viewpoints on the topic. They were looking for answers to questions that were being asked in the Church. Some of the questions were:

- *What does it mean to be covered?*
- *Why do we need a covering?*
- *Isn't Jesus the only covering I need?*

After half an hour of discussing these questions and offering suggestions for a solution, we had an agreement. The agreement was that, as leaders, we need to speak the same terminology. By doing this, we can clearly communicate what we intend to say. Collectively, the decision was made that we would no longer use the term *Apostolic Covering.* Our agreement was that, instead, we would use the term *Apostolic Alignment.*

Since that gathering of leaders, there has been agreement and revelation about what apostolic alignment means for the Body of Christ. How exciting to live in a time when the Lord is raising up mature leaders who work together to bring harmony and understanding to the Lord's people!

## Apostolic alignment

Apostolic alignment is a relationship that may be new to some people. Apostles and apostolic leaders are part of the restoration that is occurring around the world. The Early Church had leaders with different functions who led God's people. All five of the ascension gift ministries functioned in church life. Believers believed that salvation came through faith in the finished work of Jesus through His death, burial, and resurrection. *All* believers, not just spiritual leaders, operated in signs and wonders.

Much that was in the Early Church was lost during the Dark Ages. A leader named Constantine decided that Christianity was the best religion for his people during the 300s AD. We do not know whether he was a Christian. He merely chose Christianity as a good religion. Religious leaders were given tax-exempt status. Constantine didn't want to lose a lot of tax money. Therefore, to minimize the lost tax revenue, he put the poorest, most uneducated people into positions of leadership in the churches.

Most church leadership was led by people without a born-again spirit. Without personal salvation, the supernatural power of the Holy Spirit didn't have a born-again spirit to operate through. As a result, the fiery presence of the Lord was absent in most churches for many years. It was not until the 1500s when restoration began, initiated by a Catholic monk, Martin Luther, who had a revelation that salvation was only attained by faith and not by works.

Since that time, God has been restoring much that was lost in His Church. He is restoring the lost leadership functions to His Church. The 5-fold, ascension gift ministries were lost but are now restored to the Church. The Lord desired those gifts to function, not just for the Early Church, but also for today. When Jesus ascended to Heaven, after his death, burial, and resurrection, He gave gifts to His Church.

> He gave some as apostles, and some as prophets, and some as evangelists, and some as pastors and teachers, for the equipping of the saints for the work of service, to the building up of the body of Christ.
>
> Ephesians 4:11-12

The word for *equipping* in these verses is the Greek word *katartizo*. Dr. Ron Cottle explains the meaning of that Greek word in his booklet, *Apostolic Alignment*.

> The overriding sense of this word group, then, is not to equip by supplying armor, or merely enhancing spiritual development (edifying). Rather, it is to put a thing into its appropriate position. Therefore, to establish or set, to ordain or commission, to fit or align, even to adjust or

adapt are tasks much nearer to the essence of *katartizo* than to equip…

When highly gifted individuals are misplaced, when individuals with distinct callings are unable to embrace their passion or calling, the ensuing weakness causes a debilitating effect on the entirety of a ministry sphere. Thus, proper alignment is crucial to effective ministry.[1]

Having an apostolic relationship with the right apostle affects your identity and your destiny. The apostle is gifted to see potential in you that you may not see in yourself. The alignment with that apostle helps shift you into the right position. Positioning unlocks your potential for reaching your destiny. Allow the Lord to align you in an apostolic relationship. Your life will forever be changed!

**Apostolic alignment releases vision.**
One advantage of apostolic alignment is experiencing fresh vision for your future. Apostolic leaders live in the future. They continually look to see the next thing God wants to do on Earth. Alignment with these leaders propels a person into the destiny God has planned for their life. Otherwise, a person can live in the familiar without reaching God's potential for their life.

Fresh vision imparted by apostolic alignment prevents personal "tunnel vision" in life. "Where there is no vision, the people are unrestrained" (Proverbs 29:18). The word *unrestrained* means to let go or to let loose.[2] An example of that can be found in the story of God's people wandering in the desert after they left Egypt. While Moses was on the mountain receiving the word of the Lord, Aaron allowed the people to run wild and engage in idolatrous behavior. (See Exodus 32:25.) The people lost the

---

[1] Ronald E. Cottle, *Apostolic Alignment, An Intensive Word Study* (Columbus, GA: REC Ministries, 2017), pp. 12-13.

[2] Spiros Zodhiates, *Hebrew – Greek Key Word Study Bible, New American Standard Bible* (La Habra, CA: Lockman Foundation, 2008), p. 1997.

vision of where God was taking them. Without the vision for their destiny, they reverted to Egyptian culture from their past. The Message Bible encourages believers to have clear vision in their walk with the Lord.

> If people can't see what God is doing, they stumble all over themselves; But when they attend to what he reveals, they are most blessed.
> Proverbs 29:18 MSG

Vision stretches us out of our comfort zone. It helps a person see beyond their own circumstances. Apostolic alignment will challenge a person to enlarge their vision. The person experiences a "pioneering spirit" rather than becoming a "settler." The pioneering spirit catapults the person to new levels of increase, exploits, and success in their God-given pursuit of destiny!

**Release wrong alignments.**
Wrong alignments can keep a person in an old place. These alignments may be friends or acquaintances. Some of these relationships never see where the Lord is taking you. They see you where you were in the past. Some of these relationships may actually be toxic. Toxic relationships are always in need of repair. You fix the relationship today and discover that, by tomorrow, it again needs repair.

Much time and energy can be wasted trying to fix something that cannot be fixed. Realize that some relationships are only for a season. They may not be lifelong connections. Also, not all relationships are covenant relationships. Often a person attempts to draw people into a deep heart relationship. The other person may not have the same commitment to the relationship.

Be willing to release relationships that are toxic. Forgive for any wrong words or actions they have done. Allow the Spirit of God to heal any place of pain or disappointment in your heart.

Do what I heard someone say years ago: "Get around people who celebrate you, not those who only tolerate you!" Now, you are ready for right alignment for your destiny!

**Alignment is not control.**
Apostolic alignment does not infer control over a person's life. A good leader respects man's free will to cooperate. The leader can bring correction and advice but allows the believer to exercise his own faith. The leader should always help the believer walk in joy and not in defeat.

Be careful in establishing an apostolic relationship. The relationship should be with those who share a common vision and destiny. I once heard someone say, "Don't ever align with someone who does not love you." A person who loves you will not abuse you. The person who loves you does not put limits on your potential. The person who loves you wants you to go farther in your potential than they have gone in their own giftings. They will not be jealous of your progress. That leader will celebrate every step of progress that you make!

**Destiny requires right positioning.**
Right alignment has the potential of shifting a person into the right *position* so they can fulfill their destiny. A wonderful example is found in the biblical story of Ruth. The Book of Ruth helps us see how to get rightly aligned for our God-given assignment in life.

A man named Elimelech moved his family to Moab during a time of famine. He was looking for prosperity and blessings. However, he looked in the wrong place. After moving his family from the place of promised blessings, Elimelech and both of his sons died. The place of hope turned to a place of death and disappointment.

Naomi, the widow of Elimelech, had to make a choice to stay in the place of lack or move to a new place for her God-given assignment. Bethlehem was the place where God promised blessings. Moab was not where Naomi needed to be for her future! She made the decision to do whatever was necessary to be where God was releasing His blessings. She knew she must be rightly positioned to fulfill her destiny.

Naomi is a type or picture of apostolic leadership. Apostolic leaders are willing to take risks and break out of old limitations. These leaders allow the Spirit of the Lord to guide them forward rather than being captured by the limitations or the circumstances around them. Their passion is to be in the will of the Lord.

**Decisions affect destiny.**

Naomi's daughters-in-law, Orpah and Ruth, also had to choose where they would be positioned for their future. Both women had married the sons of Elimelech and Naomi. The sons both died and left them as widows. Would they stay in their familiar country, or would they take a risk and follow Naomi into unknown territory? Destiny seekers are faced with the same decision. Are they willing to align with an apostolic leader and go into unfamiliar territory, or settle in the familiar place?

Orpah initially decided to follow Naomi. (See Ruth 1:14-15.) After realizing the consequences of that decision, she chose, instead, to stay in the old place. The risks and the uncertainty of the unknown created too much fear in her. Many believers make that same decision today.

Ruth, however, made the firm decision to follow Naomi to the new place. Even after Naomi urged her to follow her sister-in-law back to the familiar, Ruth refused to leave her apostolic leader.

> Ruth said, "Do not urge me to leave you or turn back from following you; for where you go, I will go, and where you lodge, I will lodge. Your people shall be my people, and your God, my God.

"Where you die, I will die, and there I will be buried. Thus may the Lord do to me, and worse, if anything but death parts you and me."

Ruth 1:16-17

Ruth aligned herself apostolically for her next season in life. She realized that she would never get to her destiny alone.

## Favor through apostolic alignment

Naomi and Ruth had to believe for a better tomorrow than what they were experiencing today. Their faith put a demand on the circumstances to change. Like Ruth and Naomi, you are not demanding God. Your faith is demanding that the circumstances change.

What is a promise or vision that the Lord has given for your destiny? You are warring for the manifestation of that promise. The promise of God in your prophetic word now becomes part of your apostolic warfare and arsenal! Faith will make the warfare effective. Your faith now reaches a new level in your apostolic alignment. Like Ruth, you will go where you have never been before!

Ruth "happens" to find herself in the field of Boaz. (See Ruth 2:3.) Boaz was a relative of Naomi. Since Ruth was aligned with Naomi, she found favor in that place. Favor is released by being rightly aligned! Favor opens doors to the future. Favor causes the release of financial blessings and inheritance to be restored. Favor causes destiny to be fulfilled!

## Right alignment releases destiny.

The most unlikely people can be rightly aligned to receive the blessings of God in this new season. Ruth was an unlikely person. She was a Moabite, not a Hebrew. She was outside the covenant root that was destined to receive from the Lord. Boaz was also an unlikely person to receive God's blessings. He had finances but was not a Hebrew. He descended from Rahab the prostitute. (See Matthew 1:5.)

Ruth apostolically aligned with Naomi. That alignment brought favor for Ruth with Boaz, which resulted in marriage. Two very unlikely people were now rightly aligned to receive God's blessings! For Ruth, the days of living in lack as a widow were replaced with financial blessings, the inheritance of a son, and God's designed destiny for her life.

Through Ruth, the line of David was released. Through that line, ultimately, Jesus came into the world! The most unlikely persons, and the ones who were, by religious standards, outside the covenant of God, allowed the Spirit of God to lead them. They apostolically aligned themselves for their new season and changed history!

Alignment is powerful! You may feel that you are the most unlikely person to walk in your life's destiny. Watch what the Lord does in your life as you are positioned in right apostolic alignment! Like Ruth and Boaz, you can be a history changer!

# DISCUSSION QUESTIONS

1. Why is the term Apostolic Alignment a better term than Apostolic Covering?
2. What happened during the Dark Ages to cause the Church to lose the supernatural manifestations of the Holy Spirit?
3. Give an example of the result of loss of vision.
4. Describe a good apostolic leader.
5. How does right alignment release favor?
6. What are some of the blessings that are released in a right alignment?

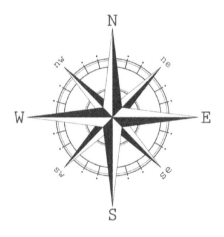

# CHAPTER 11

# Wealth for Destiny

The mansion was breathtaking! We stood looking at the Biltmore Estate for a long time before entering the massive home. The mansion was built during the late 1800s as a summer home for George W. Vanderbilt (1862-1914). The luxurious home is in Ashville, North Carolina. Biltmore Estate is considered the largest private residence in the United States.

Vanderbilt was a member of one of the wealthiest families in the United States. His family acquired a mass fortune through steamboats, railroads, and various business enterprises.

Generational wealth allowed George and his descendants to impact the world long after their lives ended. His descendants continue to operate Biltmore today. Their lives are a testimony of how generational wealth can be used as a powerful philanthropic means for making the world a better place. Visitors from around the world flock to Biltmore Estate each year to view the Chateauesque-style home with its massive collection of books, artwork, and park-like landscaping. It is a historic example of the Gilded Age mansions.

**Wealth defined**

The Vanderbilt family had huge amounts of financial wealth. However, not all wealth is money. Money is part of wealth but not limited to money. Webster defines wealth as "much money or property or affluence."[1] I wrote in my book, *Becoming a Wealth Creator*, about the Hebrew definition of wealth.

> In the Bible, one of the Hebrew definitions for the word *wealth* is *chayil*. Chayil is defined as an army, wealth, strength, or a company of soldiers. [2] God has a strong army of spiritual soldiers rising with wealth and riches to fulfill God's Kingdom purposes on Earth. How awesome that you and I can be part of this great company of Kingdom men and women living at this time in history![3]

---

[1] Michael Agnes, Editor in Chief, Webster's New World College Dictionary (New York, NY: Macmillan USA, 1997), p. 1620.

[2] James Strong, *Hebrew Dictionary of the Old Testament* (McLean, VA: MacDonald Publishing), p. 39.

[3] Barbara Wentroble, *Becoming a Wealth Creator* (Argyle, TX: International Breakthrough Ministries, 2019), pp. 14-15.

## Influence through wealth

One of the purposes of wealth is influence. Influence can either be good or bad. We frequently hear how some wealthy people donate money to those they can influence for antibiblical purposes. As a result of their sizeable donations, the donor can spread their ideas or get groups to agree with their evil ideology. I remember speaking in a nation led by a wealthy political leader. Most of the people in that nation were poor. The leader would pay a small amount of money to the citizens when they came to his political rallies. Although the amount of money paid was small, the people were influenced. Any amount of money was better than what they had! They continued voting the leader into office whether they agreed with his policies or not. They were influenced by the politician's wealth!

God desires His people to be influencers for Kingdom purposes. The Bible records the stories of many people who had wealth and were able to influence people for God's purposes. Abraham was a wealthy man. "Abram was very rich in livestock, in silver and in gold" (Genesis 13:2). He was able to travel and meet with the Pharoah of Egypt. Later, he built altars to God and became the "father of a multitude of nations." (See Genesis 17:5) God promised that Abraham's influence for righteousness would be so great that all the nations on Earth would be blessed. His destiny included wealth that gave him influence for God's purposes on Earth. Believers are still influenced today when they read the story of Abraham's life. His destiny included wealth that would be used to influence people for righteousness through the generations!

## Philanthropy

Wealth is necessary for most philanthropic endeavors. I often hear people describe a vision they have for helping the poor, building a facility for single moms, developing a resort for leaders to have a place for refreshing and rest, and many other worthy causes. The only thing that keeps them from fulfilling those desires is money. These people sense that philanthropic endeavors are part of their destiny.

Forbes magazine reported that Warren Buffet has donated the most money as a philanthropist in the United States. As of 2020, he donated $48.2 billion in his 91 years of life![4] There is a difference between charity and philanthropy. Charity is usually associated with giving to meet a short-term goal. Providing clothing for the homeless during the winter can be considered charity. Philanthropy is more long-term. The goal is usually to help society or groups be successful through projects that affect society for a long period of time. An example could be the building of a library or a hospital. The donors have a deep desire to solve problems to improve human welfare.

A person can not only donate money but also donate time or talents to become a philanthropist. The person loves people and has a desire to make life better for them. Maybe God has put the desire for helping others and helping society in your heart. Start where you are. Find a cause that is dear to your heart. Begin by donating time and work. You will then want to give finances to help that cause. Let the Lord expand your vision for philanthropy. It is part of your destiny!

## Political power

Wealth is often used as political power. It is easy to look back through history and recognize the influence of wealth on American politics. An example is President John F. Kennedy. He was the 35th president of the United States. Kennedy was born into a prominent, wealthy family with political connections. Kennedy attended prestigious schools during his younger years. His humor, charm, and father's money propelled him forward in political life. Corruption and immoral practices were prominent in the family. Still, the wealth propelled the family to a place of

---

[4] https://www.investopedia.com/terms/p/philanthropy.asp.

influence. Generational wealth was an ingredient that helped President Kennedy step into his destiny at a young age.

People do not necessarily need large sums of money to gain political power. They may need to connect with others who have the money for campaigns and other tasks necessary for gaining political influence. Don't allow the lack of finances to stop you when you know that politics is part of your destiny. Ask the Lord for the right connections to those who have the finances to support you.

Esther in the Old Testament may not have had great wealth. She was an orphan. Yet, God promoted her as Queen. She affected the destiny of a nation through her political power. Esther's wealth of influence created a generational inheritance for Jewish people. Your destiny may include affecting your city or your nation through political power. Like Esther, you can use your wealth of influence to create a good inheritance for generations to come. Allow the Lord to use your influence in politics to shift you into your God-given destiny! Generations will be affected by your political wealth!

**Kingdom wealth**
Wealth is needed to accomplish Kingdom ventures. How wonderful that the Lord promises His people the ability to create wealth.

> You shall remember the Lord your God, for it is
> He who is giving you power to make wealth, that
> He may confirm His covenant which He swore
> to your fathers, as it is this day.
> Deuteronomy 8:18

With the wealth people create, it is possible to arrive at the destiny God planned for their lives.

Andrew Carnegie (1835–1919) was a man who used wealth to fulfill his destiny. He went from "rags to riches" during his lifetime. He was born in Scotland to a family that experienced poverty. Hoping to find a better life, his father moved the family to the United States and settled in Allegheny, Pennsylvania. The family lived in two rooms above a relative's weaving shop. His father ran the business but saw it fail. Once again, the family experienced poverty.

Young Carnegie worked long hours and physically-challenging jobs as a teenager. However, he loved books and devoured them during those years. Later, he pursued various business ventures that affected people around the world. One of his business ventures was the Carnegie Steel Corporation. That corporation became the largest steel manufacturing company in the world.

Carnegie wrote *The Gospel of Wealth* which articulated his desire to use wealth for the benefit of others. He became one of the wealthiest and most famous industrialists of his day. His passion was to use wealth for helping others have a better life. One of his quotes speaks to his heartfelt cry: "To try to make the world in some way better than you found it is to have a noble motive in life."[5]

Carnegie did not allow his life of poverty to keep him from pursuing wealth. He realized that wealth is needed to help the less fortunate. Wealth is needed to give people a better life. Wealth is not merely for selfish purposes. Wealth is for the good of humanity!

Although Carnegie may not have understood Kingdom, he had a heart to create wealth to help humanity. You can begin your journey toward wealth creation today. What Kingdom causes do you dream about? Are those causes part of your destiny? Begin to create short-term goals for wealth creation. Be faithful in the small things so God can increase your wealth for Kingdom causes!

---

[5] https://www.carnegie.org/interactives/foundersstory/#!/

## Breaking wrong mindsets concerning wealth

Jewish people understand that God desires for them to have wealth. They believe that wealth is a good thing. Steven Silbiger explains the Jewish mindset and their pursuit of wealth in his book, *The Jewish Phenomenon*.[6]

> According to the New Testament, the Christian world has, at best, an ambivalent attitude toward money and wealth...
>
> For Jews, on the other hand, wealth is a good thing, a worthy and respectable goal to strive toward. What's more, once you earn it, it is tragic to lose it. Judaism has never considered poverty a virtue. The first Jews were not poor, and that was good. The Jewish founding fathers, Abraham, Isaac and Jacob were blessed with cattle and land in abundance. Asceticism and self-denial are not Jewish ideals.

Christians, on the other hand, have a different mindset. They often use scriptures to justify the lack of wealth. Some scriptures that are used to keep believers in a poverty mindset are below.

> Again I say to you, it is easier for a camel to go through the eye of a needle, than for a rich man to enter the kingdom of God.
>
> Matthew 19:24

> No servant can serve two masters; for either he will hate the one, and love the other, or else he will hold to one, and despise the other. You cannot serve God and mammon.
>
> Luke 16:13

---

[6] Steven Silbiger, *The Jewish Phenomenon* (Lanham, MD: M. Evans, 2009), pp. 12-13.

> For the love of money is a root of all sorts of evil, and some by longing for it have wandered away from the faith, and pierced themselves with many a pang.
>
> 1 Timothy 6:10

It is easy to see in these scriptures that the Bible is talking about heart issues. A person can have wealth, but at the same time, the person must keep their heart following after God. How important it is to remember that it was God that gave the person the ability to get wealth. Wealth is not limited to personal needs but is to meet the needs of humanity. Believers' mindsets must shift from the wrong interpretation of a few scriptures to a proper understanding of the entire Bible!

Another mindset concerning wealth that needs to change is a poverty mindset. I wrote about this malady in my book, *Becoming a Wealth Creator*.

> Poverty comes from a root word that means "small means" or "scarceness." A mindset of poverty keeps a person under a canopy of despair. Often the person feels they will never amount to anything. They don't have hope of ever getting a break. The person feels that others may get ahead, but life has them trapped in a place where they cannot escape.[7]

How sad to see Christians living far beneath the blessings that God promised for those who follow Him! Your destiny is not trapped in a place where there is no escape! God's will is for you to prosper.

---

[7] Barbara Wentroble, *Becoming a Wealth Creator* (Argyle, TX: International Breakthrough Ministries, 2019), p. 54.

Beloved, I pray that in all respects you may prosper and be in good health, just as your soul prospers.

3 John 2

A poverty mindset can be the result of a wounded soul. A person may have experienced personal failures or endured broken relationships, both of which may have significantly and negatively affected their mind, soul, and emotions. The person may feel unworthy. Consequently, when the soul is not prospering, the ability to comprehend and strategically pursue personal prosperity is very challenging. Finding a good counselor or mentor can be a valuable asset in breaking a poverty mindset.

**Giving to break a poverty mindset**
I found in my life that the key to breaking a poverty mindset is giving. I believe in responsible handling of money. I also believe that part of that responsibility involves giving to God and giving to others.

When I give tithes, firstfruit offerings, alms, and seed offerings, I am giving something of myself for God to bless. If I do not give, there is nothing for God to bless. A blessing is promised with each type of giving. Deeper understanding of the blessings of giving is found in my book, *Becoming a Wealth Creator.*[8] The following are the blessings:
Tithe (Malachi 3:10-11)
- Giving after a person receives wages or income.
- The devourer is rebuked by God.
- God opens the windows of Heaven and pours out a blessing until it overflows.
Firstfruit (Proverbs 3:9-10)
- Given in faith before the harvest comes in.
- No amount mentioned in the Bible.

---

[8] Ibid.

117

- Abundant blessings on all that follows the giving.

Alms (Proverbs 19:17 TPT)
- Give to the less fortunate.
- God gives back dollar for dollar.
- Always have a heart to help the needy.

Seed (2 Corinthians 9:6-7)
- Motivation for seed giving is great faith.
- Done out of joy and gratitude to the Lord.
- Blessings of increase and multiplication.

Giving opens the door for the creation of wealth for your destiny. My life has been radically changed through using the key of giving. I learned years ago that I could not stop giving during an economic downturn. The amount of giving may change during a financially difficult place. However, giving must continue to break a person out of the place of lack. Your destiny awaits you as you are faithful in giving!

**Battle for wealth**

Creating wealth for destiny is not free from difficulty. There is a battle to create wealth and then to keep from losing wealth. Life is not perfect, and people don't always make right decisions. Getting around others who know how to manage wealth is valuable. You can learn from those who have experience in the financial realm.

Read books on wealth. Knowledge is a valuable asset. Study the Bible and what it says about wealth. Ask the Lord to open your eyes and give you revelation. Knowledge about wealth and knowledge of the Bible will prepare you for success as you pursue your destiny. You will be prepared to win the battle for your wealth.

There is an enemy who wants to stop you from reaching your destiny. "The thief comes only to steal, and kill, and destroy; I came that they might have life, and might have *it* abundantly" (John 10:10). With the Word of the Lord in your heart and in your mouth, you are battle-ready! Stand strong against the enemy and keep pursuing your destiny as you create wealth for Kingdom purposes!

# DISCUSSION QUESTIONS

1. Give a simple definition of wealth.
2. Describe a biblical character that had wealth.
3. How can wealth be used for Kingdom purposes?
4. What is a philanthropist?
5. Describe the dream in your heart that requires finances to fulfill that dream.
6. What are the blessings of at least two types of giving?

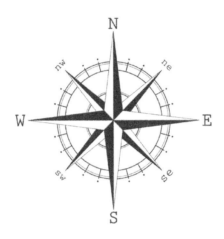

# CHAPTER 12

# Destiny Creates a Legacy

1787! A memorable year for the United States! The Constitution of the United States was written that year. The document established America's government and fundamental laws. It also established certain rights for citizens of America. The Constitution was signed on September 17, 1787, by the delegates to the Constitutional Convention in Philadelphia. The United States Constitution is the longest surviving charter that has been written for government. How powerful to read the first three words of the Preamble to the

Constitution: *We the People*! Those words declare the government of the United States exists to serve the people of the nation.

The founding fathers of the Constitution worked tirelessly to achieve the goal of government serving the people. They attempted to keep as much sovereignty and independence as possible for the individual states. Their desire was the national government would handle the most important functions of the nation that the individual states could not handle.

What a document! What a legacy for the citizens of the United States! The document was not easily written. The Constitution was finalized after many long, and often heated, discussions. Yet, after over 200 years, the Constitution remains the document for guiding this nation's government. The founders were not merely writing a document. They were creating a legacy for generations yet to be born!

**Define legacy**
What, then, is legacy? Oxford's English Dictionary defines legacy in a couple of ways.

- A gift by will, especially of money or other personal property.
- Something transmitted by or received from an ancestor or predecessor or from the past.[1]

A legacy of money can be left for future generations. Usually, the amount of money or other assets are mentioned in the predecessor's will. Having a will is vital for a person's desire to be fulfilled after their death. Without a will, the state often receives the assets. A person is never too young to have a will. Unexpected tragedies can happen. The will secures the person's desires and their assets.

---

[1] https://www.google.com/search?q=define+legacy&rlz=1C1EJFA_enUS6 90US690&oq=&aqs=chrome.1.35i39i362l8.109659j1j7&sourceid=chrome& ie−UTF 8.

A woman I knew died a few years ago. She worked but lived a very frugal life. When she died, no one from her church or among her friends knew anything about her relatives. There was no way to even contact them about the death. Friends from her church sorted through her belongings. They dispersed the collections of items, hoping they were doing it the way she would have wanted. The church paid for her funeral and memorial service. She was a very private person and kept personal information secretive.

Sometime later, a discovery was made concerning her finances. Someone discovered that she had an established fund from a previous employer with over $100,000! The lady could have used the money to have a better lifestyle. She could also have left the funds in a will to her church or to friends. However, there was no will. So sadly, all the funds went to the state!

A legacy could have been made to honor this wonderful person's life. Finances could have been designated for scholarships or many other endeavors for the next generation. Her own educational background was that of a teacher. How sad! A life well-lived but no legacy to honor that life!

**Biblical legacy**
The Bible urges believers to create a legacy. The following verses reveal that God is interested in the way we handle money and the way we prepare for the future.

> A good man leaves an inheritance to his children's children.
> Proverbs 13:22 NKJV

> The rich rule over the poor, and the borrower is slave to the lender.
> Proverbs 22:7 NIV

Helping young people understand the handling of money prepares them to be successful in life. Teaching them to prioritize the spending of money has long-term effects. Too often people spend money for current satisfaction without planning for a prosperous future. Something as simple as training them to always save a portion of what they earn for emergencies or future endeavors is such an important priority. Through saving, they will understand the personal sacrifices necessary to create a legacy.

The Bible speaks honestly about the connection of debt and the debtor. Many people have great Kingdom visions for their future. Yet, debt can rob them of their dreams. Getting free from debt can move a person toward the fulfillment of their destiny. Freedom from debt can also affect your loved ones after you are gone. Do your best to leave a stable financial situation for your family.

Legacy not only involves money, but it also involves leaving an impact on the lives of others. Your influence can continue through the generations. Reflect on the current opportunities in your life to have a positive influence on the generation coming behind you. May the future generations remember your life was not lived in vain.

Apostle Paul understood the importance of leaving a godly legacy. Some people believe he was the greatest example of a Christian missionary and theologian who ever lived. He was often referred to as the "Apostle to the Gentiles." Apostle Paul overcame tremendous obstacles in life, yet he was more responsible than anyone else for the spreading of Christianity throughout the Roman Empire. Apostle Paul pressed toward that goal so that he would win the prize of fulfilling his destiny on Earth.

> Brethren, I do not regard myself as having laid hold of it yet; but one thing *I do*: forgetting what *lies* behind and reaching forward to what *lies* ahead, I press on toward the goal for the prize of the upward call of God in Christ Jesus.
>
> Philippians 3:13-14

**Biblical characters who left a legacy**

Throughout the Bible, we read about great heroes of the faith who left a legacy for future generations. Moses was a leader who left a legacy for the Hebrew nation. He spent time training a young man by the name of Hoshea. The Hebrew name Hoshea means "salvation."[2]

When Moses would go into the Tent of Meeting, Hoshea stayed outside near the tent. He wanted to experience what he saw in the life of his spiritual father. Hoshea was also with Moses when Moses climbed Mount Sinai. He saw the glory of God and the power of God on the Mount. His life would never be the same after that experience of God's glory!

Moses changed Hoshea's name to Joshua after he toured the Promised Land, because Hoshea had such great faith that the land could be possessed by his nation. By accepting and embracing his new name, Hoshea received a new identity for his new season. No longer would Hoshea be a warrior under the leadership of Moses. Now, he would have the assignment of leading God's people forward to possess their inheritance. Joshua means "YAHWEH is my salvation."[3] The legacy of the faithfulness of God in Moses's life became a legacy of the same faithfulness of God for Joshua and the following generations!

> Moses My servant is dead; now therefore arise, cross this Jordan, you and all this people, to the land which I am giving to them, to the sons of Israel. Every place on which the sole of your foot treads, I have given it to you, just as I spoke to Moses.
>
> Joshua 1:2-3

Another example in the Bible is the legacy Apostle Paul imparted when he instructed his spiritual son, Timothy.

[2] https://www.behindthename.com/name/hoshea.

[3] https://www.behindthename.com/name/joshua.

The things which you have heard from me in the presence of many witnesses, these entrust to faithful men, who will be able to teach others also.

2 Timothy 2:2

Apostle Paul understood the value of families teaching their children. God's desire is for godly children to be raised up in every generation.

This is the commandment, the statutes and the judgements which the Lord your God has commanded *me* to teach you, that you might do *them* in the land where you are going over to possess it, so that you and your son and your grandson might fear the Lord your God, to keep all His statutes and His commandments, which I command you, all the days of your life, and that your days may be prolonged.

Deuteronomy 6:1-2

Paul wanted Timothy to pour his life into not only his own generation, but also to leave a legacy that would go into the following generations. God's desire is the same today. He desires families to instruct their children in the ways of the Lord and leave a righteous legacy for the following generations.

**Modern day legacy**
Years ago, a woman wanted her family to leave a righteous legacy for succeeding generations. Susanna Wesley (1669-1742) was the mother of 19 children. Nine children died while they were infants. Four twin children died. One child was accidentally smothered by a maid. Only eight of her children were alive at the time of her death.

Life was not easy in the Wesley household. Susanna's husband left the family for over a year due to a minor disagreement. He spent time in jail. His financial dealings often created a hardship for the family. Their house burned down twice. Susanna refused to allow these difficulties to distract her. She was daily seen sitting in a chair with an apron over her head. Her times of prayer kept her strong as she spiritually influenced an active family. Nothing distracted her from the call for educating and training her children to follow the Lord.[4]

Susanna scheduled individual times with each of her children. That time was devoted exclusively to each child. She also held devotions for her children on Sunday afternoon. She felt there was not enough of God's Word preached at the local church. Her devotions exploded into the community. Soon, as many as 200 were attending her Sunday afternoon devotions.

Susanna made a difference in her children's lives. She made a difference in the lives of those who attended her Sunday devotions. The Methodist Church credits Susanna Wesley as the Mother of Methodism. That honor is amazing, considering she never preached a sermon, never published a book, and never formally started a church. Her sons, Charles and John, became powerful spiritual leaders. They launched the Methodist Church and changed the course of Christian history. They became world changers!

The legacy left by Susanna lives on today. Her faith, devotion to prayer, and Bible reading created a legacy that is still alive many years after her death. Generations are affected by this extraordinary woman. Her legacy continues to enlarge the Kingdom of God!

**Create a legacy**
How do you want to be remembered at the end of your life? Will the following generations know about your faith? Will they receive a financial blessing to know that you wanted to bless

---

[4] https://en.wikipedia.org/wiki/Susanna_Wesley.

them? It doesn't matter where you are today. You can start to build a legacy by taking that first, determined step of action.

One of the things I do in creating a legacy is to write books. These books include stories from my life experiences. I want the books to help mentor others around the world. I also want my children and grandchildren to read stories about what the Lord did in my life and the life of our family. These children will later be able to pass these stories about the family history to their succeeding generations.

The Lord planned for generations to pass on family history. When the children of Israel crossed the Jordan into their Promised Land, they erected a memorial. They were instructed to take stones out of the Jordan with which to build a memorial. Generations in the years to come would be able to talk about the mighty deeds that God did for their families. They would be reminded that God does not change. He can do mighty exploits in their families.

> Let this be a sign among you, so that when your children ask later, saying, "What do these stones mean to you?" Then you shall say to them, "Because the waters of the Jordan were cut off before the ark of the covenant of the Lord; when it crossed the Jordan, the waters of the Jordan were cut off." So these stones shall become a memorial to the sons of Israel forever."
>
> Joshua 4:6-7

Create a memorial for your family. You may not be ready to write a book. However, you may be ready to write some blogs or other documents about your life and your faith. Or you may simply record some of your life experiences. Talk about your faith and your life to your family. They probably want to hear about the way you made it through some of the struggles you faced.

You may want to consider setting up a financial inheritance. The amount is not as important as your heart to bless. Any amount will say to the inheritor that you thought about them and made plans to leave them an inheritance. While you are planning your legacy, be sure you have a valid will. Details of your wishes should be included in the will. Keep it in a safe place where the Executor of your will knows where to find it. Death is filled with emotions. Doing your part will make it less stressful for those who continue in life after you graduate to Heaven.

## Lifetime longer

Your time on Earth will probably be longer than the lifetime of your parents or grandparents. Many studies show that people today live to be 100 years old or older. What do you plan to do with the extra time you are given on Earth? Is there a way for you to begin now to create a legacy that will affect generations after you graduate to Heaven?

Many people experience their greatest achievements in their older years. Peter Drucker, a successful management consultant, wrote 22 of his 34 books after the age of sixty. Boone Pickens, an American business magnate and financier, made most of his money after he was 68 years old.[5] The list of people with amazing accomplishments after "retirement" age goes on and on. Their achievements created legacies that continue to affect people around the world.

God put you on Earth to make the world a better place. Your true identity and purpose in life made you the unique person that you are. You are standing at a moment in time when your calling now defines your destiny. As you walk in your life's purpose, you will now create a legacy that will live past your lifetime. I love the way Bob Buford quotes a conversation with Os Guinness in his book, *Finishing Well.*[6]

---

[5] Bob Buford, *Finishing Well* (Grand Rapids, MI: Zondervan, 2011), p. 252.
[6] Ibid, p. 247.

"When we think about the Christian view of calling," he said, "I think it's important to recognize that *we can retire from our jobs, but we can never retire from our calling.* Calling gives us our sense of task or responsibility, right up to the last day we spend on earth, when we will go to meet the Caller. I think that gives life incredible value, and therefore the prosperity of finishing well is that we continue to have a strong sense of responsibility and engagement that makes each day we live enormously important."

My prayer for you is that you finish well in your calling and destiny on Earth. May Earth be a better place because you lived a life knowing your true identity in the Lord. My heart for you is that you continue pursuing your God-given purpose in life. May the fulfillment of your destiny create a legacy that lives through future generations. You were born for this moment in history! Let your heart and spirit be filled with the joy of knowing that your life is making a difference for people not even yet born!

# DISCUSSION QUESTIONS

1. Give a definition of legacy.
2. Why is having a will important?
3. What does the Bible say about inheritance?
4. What are a couple aspects of a legacy?
5. What is one way that you can begin to create a legacy for your family?
6. What is a current estimate for many people's lifetime on Earth?

# Breakthrough Resources

www.BarbaraWentroble.com

**Anointing Oils**
Breakthrough Anointing Oil
Council Room Anointing Oil

**Breakthrough Books**
You Are Anointed with Fire
*Igniting Supernatural Power*

Becoming A Wealth Creator
*Advancing into Kingdom Prosperity*

Fighting for Your Prophetic Promises
*Receiving, Testing and Releasing Your Prophetic Word*

Praying with Authority
*How to Release the Authority of Heaven*

Prophetic Intercession
*Unlocking Miracles and Releasing the Blessings*

Releasing the Voice of the Ekklesia
*Your Voice Can Change Earth*

Removing the Veil of Deception
*How to Recognize Lying Signs,*
*False Wonders, and Seducing Spirits*

## Council Room of the Lord Book Series

Accessing God's Healing Glory
Accessing the Power of God
Accessing Your Prophetic Gift

*Encourages believers to press into the Lord's Council Room
to receive Holy Spirit empowerment that is ushering in a
powerful movement for the Kingdom of God.*

## School of Practical Intercession

Advancing and Strengthening Your Intercession Gift
*10-Month, Multi-Year Courses (January-October) via Zoom Video
Conferencing. Graduates Receive Certificate of Completion
and Commissioning at Annual Gathering.*

## Monthly Meetings & Annual Gathering

Free Monthly Equipping Meeting
Monthly School of Practical Intercession Training
Annual Gathering of Breakers

# About the Author

**Barbara Wentroble** is founder and president of International Breakthrough Ministries (IbM). She is a strong apostolic leader, gifted with a powerful prophetic anointing. Ministering with cutting-edge teaching and revelation, a powerful breaker anointing is released. Giftings and anointings are activated in ministers, business leaders, and individuals for the purpose of fulfilling their destiny.

Barbara leads an apostolic network of visionary leaders globally. She empowers leaders to succeed in their God-given assignments. Barbara conducts leadership conferences that emphasize transformation through God's grace and power in cities and regions. She has been involved in the global prayer movement since the 1990s and travels around the world.

Recently Barbara launched the School of Practical Intercession, with graduates receiving Certificates of Completion and formal Commissioning at the end of each completed year. She is the author of fourteen books. These books include *You Are Anointed with Fire, Becoming a Wealth Creator, Releasing the Voice of the Ekklesia, Prophetic Intercession, Praying With Authority, Removing the Veil of Deception, Fighting for Your Prophetic Promises,* and *Freedom from Deception.*

Barbara and her husband, Dale, reside in Lantana, Texas. They are parents of three adult children and eight grandchildren.

**Barbara's contact information:**
**Website:** www.BarbaraWentroble.com
**Email:** Info@BarbaraWentroble.com
**Mailing Address:** PO Box 109, Argyle, Texas 76226
**Office Phone:** (940) 735-1005

39630087R00075